M000314518

Finding
Father
Finding
Wholeness

....
HEALING THE HEART'S DEEPEST PAIN

GREG VIOLI

Finding Father, Finding Wholeness – Healing The Heart's Deepest Wounds
Copyright © 2016 Greg Violi.

All rights reserved.

No part of this publication may be reproduced, stored in a retrieval system or transmitted in any way by any means, electronic, mechanical, photocopy, recording or otherwise without the prior permission of the author except as provided by USA copyright law.

All Scripture quotations are taken from the Holy Bible, King James Version, Cambridge, 1769, unless otherwise noted. Used by permission.

All rights reserved.

Published by: Der Überwinder-Verlag,
Astrid-Lindgren-Str. 8, 32107 Bad Salzuflen, Germany.
Cover Design: 2016 by Jemima Gassmann - Buro fur Grafik Design
Book Design: 2016 by "THERISMOS" Sp. z o.o.,
ul. Sztabowa 32, 50-984 Wroclaw, Poland.

ISBN: 978-3-944038-18-6

Books are available to order from (in multiple languages):
Der Ueberwinder Verlag
Astrid-Lindgren-Str. 8
32107 Bad Salzuflen
www.ueberwinder-verlage.de

For more information about the author and this message please visit this website:
www.greg-violi.com

From this website you can contact
and schedule speaking engagements with Pastor Greg Violi.
You can also find videos and sermons from Pastor Greg Violi on the same website.

TABLE OF CONTENTS:

ACKNOWLEDGEMENTS

First of all, I want to express the deepest thanks and love to Father God for his mercy on my life. His tremendous love and compassion that has faithfully seen me through 56 years of life. Our family doctor told my mother that if he did not discover what was wrong with my body, I would not survive more than 6 hours. This was over 51 years ago. Faithful is my God and Father. Secondly, I want to express thanks to two very special people; my wife, Marie and my son Jeff. Thank you both for the many, many hours that you both put into proof-reading and editing this writing. Your help was very needed! Also, I thank every person that helped type, give financially or pray for this book to be completed. The last appreciation that I deeply want to give is to the Tabernacle of David Church that I lead in Lage, Germany. All of you are a joy to lead, fellowship with and worship the Lord together. It is truly a great adventure that we are all discovering in the very heart of Father's pure love! Thank you for the joy of being your Pastor!

ENDORSEMENTS

SURPRISE SITHOLE

It is truly a great honor and with great excitement that I get the opportunity to endorse the book of the amazing teacher and my brother in Christ, Greg Violi. Greg has an intense passion for life, and the people around the world and the word of God. He is one of the most inspiring persons I have come across in my life. Greg is a laid down lover of Christ and ultimately makes you aspire to be a better person in your pursuit for Jesus. His Revelation to the Father God and Christ has taken me to another level. Greg has one mission in life: Flow in Life with the Father's blessing. We cannot live a life well pleasing to God without the Father's blessings. One of my fondest moments of Greg was when I was reading in his book, "Called to be Kings and Priests". Let us find the comfort of what it's like to have a father's blessing. Let us be so consumed with God that nothing else matters. For me that is a true reflection of Greg's life. He is so consumed with Jesus.

Finding Father is an amazing book that will take you on a journey. This book will encourage you and leave you with a hunger to pursue more of God. Once you start reading you won't put this book down.

"It's real. That place with Him that eclipses everything you can imagine. You can't pursue it by effort.... You can only pursue it by following him as Abba Father! Come walk with him. Enjoy the journey..."

Surprise Sithole , Author of, "The Voice in the Night"
www.surprisesithole.com
www.irisrevivalchurch.com
White River, South Africa

DR. ALAN ALTMAN

Greg Violi has fresh revelation and life changing truth about the importance of finding the Father in our life's walk. Greg has taken us into the realm of healing and wholeness, in his beautifully humble and pure approach to such a relevant subject. This book will change your life!

Alan W. Altmann (listed in *Who's Who Worldwide* directory of global leaders) (chosen 1993-94 Speaker of the Year by the *Inspirator International Magazine*) Author, motivational speaker and believer in Christ.
Web Site: www.AlanAltmann.com
Arizona, USA

DR. FRANCIS MYLES

"If you had really known me, you would know who my Father is. From now on, you do know him and have seen him!" Philip said, "Lord, show us the Father, and we will be satisfied." Jesus replied, "Have I been with you all this time, Philip, and yet you still don't know who I am? Anyone who has seen me has seen the Father! So why are you asking me to show him to you?" (John 14:7-9)

How many spiritual leaders in the Body of Christ can truly fit in the shoes of John 14:7-9? Jesus Christ who is our eternal royal high priest told His disciples that He was the physical embodiment of the heavenly Father. The genuine life-changing love and affection that was oozing out of Him towards them was how the heavenly Father felt about His earthly sons and daughters! "If you have known and seen me, you have known and seen My Father," Jesus told His disciples! To which Philip quickly responded, "Lord show us the Father!"

Then the Holy Spirit said to me, "Son there is a generation of Philips in the Body of Christ, who are crying for God's leaders to show them the Father!" This generation of sons and daughters has heard every sermon there is to hear and yet their hearts are still emotionally empty. This is because the greatest cry of every generation since the fall of Adam is not for more spell-binding sermons; it is for "fathering!"

For even if you had ten thousand others to teach you about Christ, you have only one spiritual father. For I became your father in Christ Jesus when I preached the Good News to you (1 Corinthians 4:15).

In First Corinthians 4:15, Saint Paul makes it clear that one true spiritual father is more valuable than ten thousand teachers in Christ. This is a deeply profound statement coming from the mouth of one of the most profound teachers of the Word in human history. Paul was a great teacher to the Gentiles and yet he knew that his great apostolic teaching was no match for a true "fathering spirit."

Like Jesus, Paul knew that all the great teaching in the world could never replace the need for true spiritual and natural fathering to a generation of orphans. It is not the lack of teaching that is destroying the world; it is the lack of fathering. Financial markets and entire communities are imploding because they are being led by men or women who are controlled by unhealed "father pain." God wants to intercept and reverse the devastation caused by the orphan spirit by releasing an unstoppable fathering spirit in the earth. This supernatural infusion of the fathering spirit is especially needed in the marketplace. It is desperately needed in the corridors of human government and in the boardrooms of large corporations, whose decisions affect the destinies of millions of people worldwide.

God wants to raise apostolic men and women in the global Church and in the marketplace who will take responsibility for fathering this generation of orphans into the Father's Kingdom. Pastor Greg Violi is certainly one of those Christ-like compassionate leaders with a message for all those who are looking to "Find Father and Wholeness" in their lives. His latest book is truly an antidote to much of the "Father Pain" that exists in the world today. I highly recommend it!!!

Dr. Francis Myles
Author: The Order of Melchizedek
Senior Pastor
Royal Priesthood International Embassy
Arizona, USA

CARMELA MYLES
The Father's Blessing is a must to have in your arsenal of foundational books. I highly recommend this book for every believer to have as it captures the very essence of God's longing for His children to see Him as their Heavenly Father. I have been prayed over in the past with regards

to the Father's love and blessing but have never experienced a deeper touch until Greg and Marie released the father and mother's blessings over me. I encourage you to read this book and expect healing, miracles and a renewed relationship with the Father. I truly believe that this is possible because Greg just doesn't have a revelation of the Father's heart and blessing, he is also walking in it. In my opinion, he has become a walking epistle that could impart the Blessing of the Father accompanied with an undeniable manifestation of God's presence.

Carmela Myles, Co-Pastor Royal Priesthood International Embassy
Tempe, Arizona, USA

DR. MARTIN BATANA
"A Masterpiece."
I cannot find any other word to qualify this new book of Pastor Greg Violi! This anointed Man of God reconciles the human condition with the word of God. Deeply, with a certain art, conviction and power. With him, the concept of father is restored and raised up to the highest level. It shows all different dimensions of the father's special anointing.

In fact, with Greg, the concept of father is explored in its most unexpected depths, most diverting too, at both human and spiritual levels such as a great module within the plan of God for the family. He shows that the lost godly family in Genesis is restored through true love in Jesus: Earthy family should reflect that love to realise the plan of God to save not only the people but also the family.

From the beginning to the end, the reader is lifted up by the lightning power of the Truth, the Word of God. A spiritual movement that defies physical gravity and transcends temporality and spatiality, as he enters both practical experiences and the spiritual realm. While reading this book, you will have the feeling that it talks to you directly, deeply and with powerful restorative words because it reveals even secret hidden emotions, thoughts, beliefs, or passions.

Greg Violi has succeeded in bringing back the lost fatherhood of Eden in our hearts. A highly anointed performance that could only have been inspired by the Holy Ghost. In fact, it is only the Spirit of God that can inspire such writings to someone whose own experience on the topic is not a didactic model but the catalyst of an awakening.

Beyond the fundamental relationship between the father and his children, it is the intrinsic virtue between man and God and between man and his similar that is questioned. The law of God is simplified here by a crystallization of its attributes: Prayers to be healed, to be delivered, to be restored, to be built up, to be comforted, to be taught, to be empowered. Words of hope that will bring you to the very throne of grace. Greg makes the Word of God more alive than ever. He definitely shows its facets, especially to honor God in all relationships.

With Greg Violi, the concept of father is completely stripped from the cultural and ideological mind-set. It is simply real and alive! This book is a powerful instrument of both material and spiritual progress, of the rise of the soul, strengthening of faith and sanctification of the heart. It challenges the conscience, breaks the pride of ego, draws a figure of heavenly behaviour and restores the broken walls of godly pathways. Pastor Greg Violi brings us back to our true citizenship: Heavenly belonging and the culture of heaven.

Dr Martin Batana
Anthropologist, Sociologist and Nanophysicist
Cofounder & Chairman – The Abraham Connection, Blessed to be a blessing, E.V.
Bielefeld, Germany

SOPHIE MCLACHLAN

"As my spiritual father, Greg lives the Word, speaks the Word and carries the Word with great authority to break any barrier hindering the deep Love of the Father. His life reflects the humility and gentleness of God. Let this book draw you into the Father's embrace and let the Word come alive in your heart. Be forever changed."

Sophie McLachlan, Founder of "Awaken Love for Africa."
England

DR. GEORG SAVA

We have known Greg and his family for 11 years. As part of a Christian fellowship in the Westphalian town of Lengerich, Germany, we read about him on the internet and decided to invite him as a speaker. We didn't know that he had never been in Germany before, but on contact with him we heard, that he felt it was the leading of God to follow the call to Germany.

In accordance to this, Greg and his family visited our church in the fall of 2005 and our friendship began as well as a love for Germany which continues to increase in Greg.

The first thing that really touched us at their first visit was not only what he said, but the life we all witnessed and the acceptance and respect Greg's family had for each other, including the future son-in-law, Paul. What we saw and experienced on a practical level while being with the Violi family was then taught and shown from Scripture in the following days in the Seminar and we were blessed as a church and as a family. It's still like this today – whenever we visit the Violis, our children love to accompany us – and that's not really the case anymore when we go on other trips. So it wasn't just words, but deeds that spoke to us and blessed us.

In this sense I wish for the reader of this book, that he doesn't just take in words and information, but rather opens himself up for the working of the Holy Spirit. He is able to make these words full of life, and to bring changes in one's own heart and in the relationships to parents, children and spouses. Our nations will never change until we are first willing to allow God to change us. When we are changed, then we will start to see our spouses, our families and our nation change. Be changed as you read this book and then live it out in your life and family.

George Sava, House Church Lengerich/Westphalia, Germany
Specialist for Internal Medicine and Cardiology

CHAPTER 1
THE IMPORTANT ROLE OF FATHER

My physical Father never honored me or the work that I did. But then I got to know God. He was the best father one can imagine. He loves me and all of his children so strongly. And after I received the father's blessing my happiness was complete. My life has changed. Not only externally but especially inside me. I can feel his love, mercy, grace and loyalty clearly! Praise the Lord! I owe him so much; my whole life has changed into the positive. Thanks and honor be to him, our heavenly father!

— Jasmin, Austria

Get ready for a journey; a magnificent journey into the heart of God. The purpose of this book is that the reader might discover what Father means. There are many individuals that have no idea what it means to be a father. Even fathers many times do not realize what it is to be a father. They have been placed into that position maybe through having a baby, but they had no intention to have a child at the time that it happened. The announcement of the pregnancy came as a shock to them and they were not expecting to be a father so soon. Before someone can know what a father is, they need to enter into the very heart of the eternal Father himself. To know the Father, is to know what it means to be a father. If we turn it around, then we will think that to know an earthly father is to understand Father God. This has caused many problems in multitudes of individuals that have experienced abuse of some kind with their earthly father. Trying to know God's love through the experience of an abusive earthly father will result in confusion and frustration. Instead, knowing God's loving and pure heart will result in forgiving and loving an abusive earthly father. In this book, we will come to know the Father and in knowing Him, we will discover our wounds and will be encouraged to enter into our true self. In reading about Father God, we will learn of his tremendous plan for his children and then we will open our heart to allow Him to heal the fears, anxieties and pain that is associated with our life. To know God's heart causes one to find a new love for God and a new respect for others. The journey that you are about to take will thrill your heart, heal your heart, and prepare you for the exciting days that are ahead! Get ready for the glorious, liberating and healing journey that you are about to go on!

I will not give a lot of statistics and facts concerning single parent homes, children growing up without fathers, and etc.; there is a voluminous amount of research available for anyone that is interested to checking the statistics. I also do not desire to fill the reader's mind with knowledge. I desire to fill the reader's heart with healing, love and restoration. This book will speak directly to the heart and not just to the head giving information. Some background information seems appropriate at this point.

In the midst of marital conflict and strife, I was born on May 4th, 1959. I come from a large family with eight surviving children and thirteen pregnancies. Due to financial burdens my father had to work two jobs and I did not get to spend much time with him. I can remember waiting until midnight so that I could see him for about 10 minutes before he had to go to his second job. When I was 5 years old I was hospitalized for 52 days and I do not remember my father one time coming in to see me. My father liked to play sports, particularly soft ball and bowling and so I would always try to go with him if possible. My dad had several heart attacks and one night in January, when I was 14 years old, I kept thinking that tonight my dad's heart would stop beating. That very night, my dad's heart did stop beating and he died on the way to the hospital. This ended my short relationship with my father. At the funeral, I dreaded the thought that I would soon be looking at my father in the coffin. I wanted to stay in our attic and never come downstairs; I just simply could not face people or life at this time. All through my teenage years I was seeking one major thing, peace.

How is it that I, Greg Violi, am writing a book that deals with fathers? First of all, when we had our first born daughter Stacy, I can recall crying out to God and saying, "You must help me! I don't know how to be a father." Well, for the last 35 years I believe that I can say with God as my witness that we have had heaven on earth (Deuteronomy 11:21). In other words, the atmosphere of heaven (righteousness, peace, joy, and love) has filled our family and our home. Father God has helped us tremendously and he has taught us how to be a family and how to train our daughters in a way that is pleasing to Him. We have seen hundreds and hundreds of families and marriages healed in many nations. The Lord has also been teaching me on the role of fathers and I have seen what the blessing of a father releases into the life of the people who receive it. Lastly, I have witnessed hundreds of men develop into Godly leaders for their families.

WHY FATHER'S ROLE IS SO VITAL

The father is the source and strength of the family. It is his seed that brings forth the children. One could say that he is the source from which they come. A child derives its life from the father's seed and the child will seek to find its identity from its source of origin. Therefore, there is a longing in the heart of a child to discover its source of origin or "father". No matter how old the child is, the child is always longing to discover father, because in finding father he finds himself. The role that God has placed within a father is so great, that no one can take the father's place. It is the voice of the father that calls the child into being. The father calls forth the man out of the boy and the "father" calls forth the woman out of the girl. God the Father is the source of life in all creation, and He desires every father to reveal what He is like to his children. Earthly fathers represent the heavenly Father to their children and the world will tend to see God the same way that they see their earthly father.

A tremendous testimony to the world about God is for a father to be a godly example of kindness to his family. Philip said to Jesus, *"show us the Father and it sufficeth us"* (John 14:8). In other words, once we see the Father, this will meet our every need. Just show us the Father, is the cry of every child that is born into the world. Every earthly father has the wonderful privilege of revealing Father God to his children. Here are a few quotes that show the impact that fathers produce in their children: "He did not tell me how to live, he lived and let me watch him do it", Clarence Kellard. "It doesn't matter who my father was, it matters who I remember he was", Anne Sexton. "A truly rich man is one whose children run into his arms when his arms are empty" source unknown. "Father, to God himself we cannot give a holier name", William Wordsworth. So every child is saying within their heart, "show me the Father and it is sufficient for me," and every dad should say "can't you see Father God in me." Every child born into the world should have a good feeling about dad and each one should have a longing within them to experience their father's loving arms. I personally believe that every daughter yearns for her father to show her attention and to tell her that she is pretty and that he loves her.

MAN'S GLORIOUS DESTINY

"I and my father are one. Then the Jews took up stones again to stone him. Jesus answered them, many good works have I showed you from my Father; for which of these works do you stone me? The Jews answered him saying, for a good work we stone thee not; but for blasphemy, and because that thou, being a man, makest thyself God. Jesus answered them, is it not written in your law, I said, Ye are gods? If he called them gods, unto whom the Word of God came, and the Scripture cannot be broken, Say ye of him, whom the Father hath sanctified, and sent into the world, thou blasphemest because I said,I am the Son of God?"

(John 10: 30-36).

In answer to the rebuke and hatred of the Jews, Jesus said he and the father are one and Jesus quotes Psalms 82:6, *"I said ye are gods."* This is a very clear response to the Jews that the destiny of all men, is to reveal and manifest God in their lives. Our calling and our destiny is to reveal God himself. Revealing God first to our families and then to our world. What a tremendous privilege and honor to show all of creation what God looks like. As people observe us, they should be observing the personality of Father God through us. Our eyes, our actions, and our words should express ANOTHER, this other is the whole purpose of creation and is the meaning of what God meant when He said let us make man in our image and after our likeness. Also, if you read the context of Psalm 82, it is very clear that the *"gods"* represent the image and likeness of Father God in his attitude towards the meek, the poor, and the needy.

> *As we bring pure love into the earth, heaven is coming through us in a tangible way, but as we walk in strife and fleshly desires the kingdom of darkness is coming through us in a tangible way.*

Mankind is not just here on earth with no specific purpose. Instead, He has a very high calling that can only be fulfilled as he finds his place in the Son of God. Sonship is an idea that comes straight from God the Father's heart and all of this earthly life is teaching God's children how to reign and rule as sons and daughters of God. This is a major key to being a godly father, a man that reveals God the Father to his family. We will cover this in much greater detail throughout this book. Right after the Holy Spirit says in Psalms 82:6-7a, *"Ye are gods, and all of you are children of the Most High; then He says, "But ye shall die like men".* 1 Cor. 3:2-3 says, *"I have fed you with milk, and not with meat; for hitherto ye are not able to bear it, neither yet now are ye able. For ye are yet carnal! For whereas there is among you envying and strife, and divisions, are ye not carnal, and walk as men."* Paul is saying, when a believer that is one spirit with the risen exalted Lord (see 1 Corinthians

6:17) and seated in the heavenly places in Christ (see Ephesians 2.6), and is walking in strife and carnality; then he is living his life as an earthly mere man. He is denying the great privilege he has of being a son of God. As we bring pure love into the earth, heaven is coming through us in a tangible way, but as we walk in strife and fleshly desires the kingdom of darkness is coming through us in a tangible way. We are called to change the earth by setting our mind and affections on things above (Colossians 3:1-2) and bringing the kingdom of heaven to our earth.

If we live after our flesh (Romans 8:5-7) then we are denying our birthright, rejecting our calling, and disowning our inheritance in Christ. I will am not saying that we are equivalent to God, but I say that many of God's children have sold their birthright; just as Esau did for a bowl of soup (see Hebrews 12:16). Instead of pursuing the tremendous treasures that are given to them in the heavenly realm in Christ; they instead have chosen to settle for earthly pleasures. When Esau said, "Behold, I am at the point to die, and what profit shall be my birthright to me?" (Genesis 25:32). The actual meaning is that someday he will die. He was not saying that he's about to die now; but instead he was saying one day I will die, so what will my birthright profit me? This revealed his heart. He only considered his own selfish needs and not the millions of people that would benefit by his walking in his birthright. The god that he served was the god of this world called his own belly (Phillipians 3:19).

Millions of men have already rejected the blessings, spiritual-giftings, and eternal realities for similar worldly desires of their own fleshly mind. People not born again will live their life as a mere man. Whereas born again new creations have a much higher destiny and calling. 1 Cor. 15:41 says, *"there is one glory of the sun, and another glory of the moon, and another glory of the stars, one star differeth from another star in glory."* Even so, when Barak did not want to lead in the battle, but instead he preferred Deborah to lead and go with him; he was denying the glory that was to be given to him (see Judges 4:6-9). Every man has been called to the glory of fatherhood, the glory of leadership, and to reveal the glory of his Creator. Once again many fathers have abdicated their glorious position to their wives.

"Children's children are the crown of old men; and the glory of children are their fathers", (Proverbs 17:6). King Solomon, who wrote Proverbs, was well acquainted with the majesty, dignity, glory, and honour that a crown gives a man. Therefore, he said, the crown of a grand-father is his grand-children. At this present time (2016) I have seven diamonds in my crown. Grandchildren are the majestic crown that a grandfather wears. How many grandfathers have discarded their crown in the garbage or how many have cared and polished their crown daily? The glory of a child is his father. It is very obvious to discern if a child is carrying their glory with them, because their face will shine. To make this practical, I have listed 10 signs to show a child is carrying their glory with them.

1. They feel special when dad is with them.
2. They feel very important because dad is beside them.
3. They feel their dad can do anything and he's the best.
4. They feel that no one is as strong as their dad is.
5. They feel safe with dad.
6. They are not afraid when dad is near them.
7. They know dad will not let them down because he's there to help them.
8. The children will come into their personhood and learn to enjoy themselves as a boy or a girl.
9. They will talk with dad when other children say bad things to them.
10. They are empowered by dad's blessings through his words, thoughts, prayers, actions, and special times of just going places alone with him (dad).

My dear brother or sister, if your glory was taken from you or your glory (father) abused you, rejected you, abandoned you or hurt you; Father God will restore your glory as you continue reading this book. You are special in his eyes!

There is a certain glory for men and there is another glory for women. Some things only men can do and some things only women can do. God gave men and women certain responsibility and as they fulfil it, this becomes their glory. Some things God meant only for fathers to do; and some things for mothers. This is the hour in history when men are taking back their royal calling to be a king and a priest to the Most High God (see Revelation 1:6; 5:10). They are taking back their manhood. They are having the years that the locusts have eaten restored to them (see Joel 2:25). My brother, if you have failed, there is mercy and grace at the throne (see Hebrews 4:16). The present moment is very important, not the past or the future moment, but this present moment is the most important! The great "I AM" will fill you with his present grace to be a true man from this moment on.

What is a true man? A male individual that is indwelt by the very life of God, who shuns all passivity, embraces responsibility, pursues all of his enemies, enjoys leadership, loves and defends the poor and needy and fulfils his God given purpose. A true man is a human being that depends only on the strength and life of God, putting no confidence in his own strength. God never intended his creation to strive and struggle out of their own abilities. He always desired his creation to allow Him to live in and through them (see author's book, "The Heavenly, Victorious Life".)

Isaiah 32:2 gives God's own job description for these true men. *"And a man shall be as a hiding place for the wind and a shelter from the tempest; as rivers of water in a dry place, as the shadow of a great rock in a weary land."*

A man's presence shall be:

a. a hiding place from the wind (the wind can blow dust into your eye and it can be infected and seriously hurt)
b. A shelter from the storm (when others try to storm on your picnic (joy) the presence of a man shall be your covering to protect you).
c. Rivers of water in a dry place, (refreshing just by his coming into the room).

d. Shadow of a great rock in a desert (protection and safety in troubled times).

> *A man that is fulfilling his destiny shall be God possessed,*
> *God indwelt, God-centered, God ruled,*
> *and God's chosen man.*

Just the presence of a true man, God living inside of him, will cause him to be all of these things to his family. A man that is fulfilling his destiny shall be God possessed, God indwelt, God-centered, God ruled, and God's chosen man. The eyes of Almighty God are seeking men that He can show Himself strong on their behalf (see 2 Chronicles 16:9). *"I sought for a man, that should make up the hedge, and stand in the gap before Me for the land"* (Ezek. 22:30a). God is still seeking men that He can use as vessels. Our life is only a vapor (see James 4:14). We do not have long to decide what we will do with our life. My brother, will you be that man that the Lord is seeking now?

CHAPTER 2
FATHER WOUNDS

My name is Jenny and I would like to share with you how Gods Love changed my life. Since I was a little girl I loved Jesus, but because I experienced so much rejection in my life from my family, my church, my friends and my school I was a deep wounded girl. I really loved God, but I could never feel his love towards me, although I prayed a lot to do so. At the end of 16 years I was full of fear, insecurity, self-hatred and thought of suicide. I really believed, that I am not able to handle relationships and not worthy to be loved. With all of my heart I believed that the life here on earth is not beautiful. I said to God: "Lord, my heart is a pile of shards- nothing from my heart is still whole. Only you can heal me through a miracle."

My God and my Father was so faithful to me! He came with His love deep inside of me and drove out all the fear, all the hate and all the self-pity. God showed me His father heart through Pastor Greg many times. The Lord healed me from all Depression and broke all the lies over my life, which used to torment me every day. He laid his Hand on my wounded heart and restored it. He was so faithful to His word! Now I can say with all of my heart: Life IS beautiful! The most beautiful and the most appreciated name of God for me is Father.

– Jenny P, Germany

In this chapter, I will share few of the wounds that I have seen God heal in thousands of people that were directly related to their earthly father.

ABANDONMENT

A father's one major requirement is to be present. He does not have to be wealthy. He does not have to be good-looking. He does not have to be talented. He does not even have to be educated, strong, mechanical or intelligent; but he must be present. All those other qualities are beneficial and good, but not essential. If a father has all of the above, but he is not there for his family, they will be deeply wounded on the inside. A father can be present in his body, but still not be there in his soul. Maybe, he does not give his family time to speak with him. When he is at home, perhaps he is too pre-occupied with his work, or too tired to communicate and listen to his wife and children. Some fathers are mistreated or stressed at their job, and then they return from work and come home with a bad attitude; proceeding to take it out on their children or wife. If dad is not physically present, children will assimilate the guilt and shame of dad not being there and believe a lie that it is their own fault he is not there. Often, when a couple goes through a divorce, their children will feel it is because of something they did. Dr. James J. Lynch, has written a book called, "A Cry Unheard", (new insights into the medical consequences of loneliness). (Lynch 2000)

"He has discovered that loneliness in childhood has a major significant impact on the incidence of serious disease and premature death decades later in adulthood." (Amazon Review)

I have prayed with thousands of broken hearted children whose father abandoned them. Abandonment is a form of abuse. Abandoned children grow up feeling unwanted, unworthy, and unloved. They usually are not able to believe that God cares about them, that he loves to pour out on them gifts, and to answer their prayers.

Where did abandonment begin? It began in the Garden of Eden when our forefather Adam walked away from God. *"And the Lord God called to Adam, and said unto him, where are you?"* (Genesis 3:9).

Whatever we sow, we shall reap.

Therefore, since our first forefather abandoned God, his children have been abandoning their families ever since the garden. The seed of abandonment was sown into the heart of all of Adam's descendants. When a father abandons his family, self-hatred enters deep inside of their souls. The father is the only one that can affirm them. Only dad can make his daughter feel special because she is a girl and only dad can make his son feel special because he is a boy. Mom can comfort, nourish, and give the children a sense of well-being; but dad has the responsibility of affirming his child's gender. I believe that gender confusion is directly related to the lack of a father's affirmation.

ABUSE

Any type of abuse (physical, sexual, emotional, or mental) leaves a person traumatized. Abuse is defined by the Mosby's Medical dictionary as: any action that intentionally harms or injures another person. Abuse also encompasses inappropriate use of any substances, especially those that alter consciousness (e.g., alcohol, cocaine, methamphetamines). (Mosby, Inc 2009)

Although this definition might be good, I believe it is far too narrow. There is one major type of abuse that is almost always ignored. This abuse is when the most needed substance, love, is denied or withheld from an innocent victim. This substance that every individual must have in order to live in an appropriate, healthy way is love. We were made for love.

> *There is one major type of abuse that is almost always ignored. This abuse is when the most needed substance, love, is denied or withheld from an innocent victim.*

Our Creator is love and therefore He technically and physiologically wired and designed us to receive His nature of love. When a person receives this one essential substance; their whole being and every system will function the way they were intended to function. If a parent would withhold water or food from their children they would immediately be condemned as an abusive parent. What we fail to consider, is the vulnerable, helpless, and lowly nature of every infant and child; and how easily they can be wounded by not receiving the essential God ordained need of receiving love on a regular basis. Every little child wants their dad and mom to just hug, to kiss, and to tell them that they are special.

I have literally prayed for thousands of people that were suffering under the heavy burden of lovelessness. They had become so accustomed to not receiving this essential substance, that they did not even realize that this lack was the main cause of their pain.

One major psychological disorder is called Deprivation neurosis and this is basically the effects of not being touched. If a child is deprived of a loving, gentle, and affirmative touch, they could easily be affected with deprivation neurosis. Some of the forms of domestic violence is yelling, screaming, dishonouring, and hating one another in the privacy of your own home. This is where some Christian couples are missing God and his plan for their family. They have ignored this form of abuse and have deemed it as acceptable as long as it is in the privacy of your own home. This is totally wrong and destructive and it will always leave wounds on each family member.

The love of God must flow in two directions, through honor and blessing. To bless means to kneel down and to empower a person to prosper in life. To honor someone means to show that person they have great value, acknowledging that they have worth in the sight of God and therefore they are precious. When an individual receives honor from another person, it leaves them with an inner feeling that "I am special". God's original intention was that his creation would love, honour, and bless each other; therefore loving their neighbor as their very own self. The law of our King has always been to do to others what you would desire that they do to you. What person does not want to receive love, honor, and blessing from others?

When a child grows up in an environment that is abusive, this will leave them with great disappointments and deep seated pain, sorrow, and even death can settle down into their very soul. The more you love someone, the more that person can hurt you. For example, every daughter has a special love for her father; likewise he is supposed to cover, protect, and honor her as a special treasure that God has given to him. If this father abuses his daughter, her soul becomes traumatized and many times a spirit of trauma will enter in and continue to traumatize her emotions, memories, and body until it is driven out.

The father is the spiritual covering over his children. Once, the Lord told me that I was like an umbrella. If I have willful sins in my life, there are holes in my spiritual umbrella. When I repent of my sins, the Lord will fill in my holes and the evil one will not be able to come through my umbrella to attack my family or myself. Whenever a father abuses his precious daughter in any way, she will feel: shame, uncovered, fearful, and fragmented in her soul.

"Emotional abuse can be so serious that as Frederick Buechner describes, "a boy of twelve or thirteen who, in a fit of crazy anger and depression, got hold of a gun somehow and fired at his father, who died not right away but soon afterward. The authorities asked the boy why he had done it, he said that it was because he could not stand his father, because his father demanded too much of him, because he hated his father. And then later on, after he had been placed in a house of detention, a guard was walking down the corridor late one night when he heard sounds from the boy's room, and he stopped to listen. The words he heard the boy sobbing out in the dark were, "I want my father, I want my father".(Buechner 1985)

How sad this is, but how true. The feelings of ambivalence (hate and love) for fathers have reached an extremely high level in today's fatherless cultures all over the world. The soul of a person is longing for father's love, gentleness, and his attention. Many parents have never felt the loving, kind arms of their own father embracing them as children; so the pain that we have never been healed of is now transferred onto our own children. The unmet need within our soul, with all of our buried pains is not capable of releasing love and healing to others. Deep down we are longing for our dad to just say, "I love you", "everything is o.k.", and "you are doing a good job". Instead children often hear words of condemnation, reproach, and disappointment from their fathers. Therefore, at the very same time, while there is a deep longing for affirmation and love and there is also a deep buried anger or resentment.

> *The soul of a person is longing for father's love, gentleness, and his attention.*

Sexual abuse, especially in a daughter, will result in many female physical problems. Fear triggers the hypothalamus gland and spirits will attack the body. The invisible world of darkness is watching for an advantage to come into the souls of men (see Ephesians 4:27, 1 Peter 5:8). Wherever there is hatred, there will also be demonic spirits nearby. 1 John 3:12a says, *"Cain, who was of that wicked one"*. This is especialy true in the realm of anger. God specifically says that Cain's anger was coming from the wicked one. It is important to guard your heart when you are near an angry person, because the spirit of hate will try to defile your mind.

One time Jesus rebuked his disciples severely for wanting to call fire down on some people for rejecting Jesus. *"But he turned, and rebuked them, and said, ye know not what manner of spirit ye are of"* (Luke 9:55). If a parent doesn't ask the Lord to cleanse them of all defilement, they could easily defile their children with their words. Many good meaning parents have been agents of defilement for the evil one to dirty, defile, and shame their children. If defilement is on the inside of someone, it will come out of them through words and actions.

Prayer:
"Father God, come in Your gentle love and power with oil and wine (healing and joy) to the dear one that is reading this now. Bring healing to the deep pain they have carried from an uncaring, abusive, or absent father. Thank you father God for your nearness, great compassion, and love for this dear child of yours."

CHAPTER 3
CALLED TO BE A BLESSING

My life before the Father's Blessing:

- Traumatic events in early childhood and youth
- Many illnesses since early childhood
- A lot of hospital stays till the age of 60
- Changed my profession 3 times
- Debt – No matter how much I worked (and I worked a lot) I always ended up in debt
- Relationships broke off
- Single mum
- Fear, worry and restlessness
- Abuse, disregard/disdain, and very little recognition from other people

The effects of the Father's Blessing on my life:

I received the Father's Blessing on September 26th 2013. I will never forget this day, because my whole life changed. Two days after the Father's Blessing was given, I could feel it in my whole body and little by little, healing started to manifest.

- Spiritually, my "True Self" started to appear: a renewed and deepened inner relationship with Father God, deep rest, peace and security, a steadfast faith, joy – I just sense a covering I never had.
- Physical Healing – my physiotherapist noticed the difference straight away and inquired of me what I did. I had a different way of carrying

myself, stood upright and stood solid. For the first time in my life I felt my "inner core" and I stopped walking around as if on cotton wool. My coordination is completely healed.
- Financial Restoration – My Income changed at once! It started to grow and I am without debt for the first time in 25 years.
- Esteem, honor and recognition are now my portion. All the fears, deep cares and the restlessness are no longer there. Deep peace is inside of me together with wonderful warmth. I used to feel cold all the time!
- Family relations restored: After 22 years the relationship to the father of my son is restored and since October 2015 we are married and now we are a family! So at the age of 62 I have a brand new, blessed life with courage, trust, firm faith and joy – I have not laughed as much in my whole life as in the past two years. God, the father, Jesus Christ and the Holy Spirit be all Glory and Thanks. "

– Name withheld, Germany

Every child is longing for father to bless him even if he is 60 or 70 years old. Within every person's aching heart is a longing to have father's approval, affirmation, and blessing. If only earthly fathers could see their children in the way the heavenly Father sees them.

> *Some Christian parents are afraid to bless their child for fear that they will communicate a wrong message to them.*

The most prosperous blessed people and culture in the world is the Jewish culture. When it comes to inventions, wealth, Nobel prizes, and etc.; they have many accomplishments in all of these areas and much to rejoice in. Why is the Jewish culture so successful? I feel the main reason they are so blessed is because within the very fabric of Jewish lifestyle is a culture that is founded upon blessing. There are over 400 references to Scriptures that refer to the subject of blessing.

There is a special ceremony for Jewish boys called a Bar Mitzvah and for a Jewish girl called a Bat Mitzvah. For a boy it is to be a celebration at age 13 and for the girl, the age is 12. The first thing God did after he created man was to bless him (see Genesis 1:28). Jesus would stop on his journey and take up children in his arms and bless them (see Mark 9:36, 10.16). The last thing Jesus Christ did on earth, right as he was being taken up into the sky was to reach out and bless his disciples (see Luke 24:50, 51). Peter said in his epistle, quoting King David, if you give slander and evil talk in return for evil talk; then you cannot inherit the blessings that you are called to inherit (see 1 Peter 3:9, Psalm 34). Lastly, Jesus said on his sermon on the mount that we are to bless those that curse us (Luke 6:28).

Some Christian parents are afraid to bless their child for fear that they will communicate a wrong message to them. If a child is being rebellious, the behavior should be disciplined while the personhood of the child is to be honored. He says that we are to honor all men (1 Peter 2:17a). One way to show honor is to give blessing. The prophet Balaam was told by God that *"thou shall not curse the people; for they are blessed"* (Numbers 22:12b). Even the rebellious Israelites were blessed and God would not let the prophet Balaam curse them (see also Numbers 22:6). When Isaac saw that he had failed to bless his first born son Esau, it says that he "trembled very exceedingly" (Genesis 27:33a).

> *If a child is being rebellious, the behavior should be disciplined while the personhood of the child is to be honored.*

The very first thing that Jacob does when he sees his two grandsons was to say, *"Bring them, I pray thee, unto me, and I will bless them"* (Genesis 48:9b). He did not ask Joseph have they been good little boys so that I can impart blessings to them. No, he immediately begged Joseph to bring them to him so he could quickly bless them. He must have known that he had to take care of his crown and polish it good. *"Children's children are the crown of old men"*, (Proverbs 17:6a).

One day Thomas Edison came home and gave a paper to his mother. He told her, "My teacher gave this paper to me and told me to only give it to my mother."

His mother's eyes were tearful as she read the letter out loud to her child: Your son is a genius. This school is too small for him and doesn't have enough good teachers for training him. Please teach him yourself.

Many, many years after Edison's mother died and he was now one of the greatest inventors of the century, one day he was looking through old family things. Suddenly he saw a folded paper in the corner of a drawer in a desk. He took it and opened it up. On the paper was written: Your son is addled (mentally ill). We won't let him come to school any more.

Edison cried for hours and then he wrote in his diary: "Thomas Alva Edison was an addled child that, by a hero mother, became the genius of the century."

> ### Reverse the curse with a blessing!

My Story:

As a child growing up, I grew up under a cloud of rejection and this cloud followed me into my marriage and relationships with my children. The Lord in his mercy allowed me to see my wife and daughters the way He saw them. I can remember the first time I saw Marie through the eyes of God. She looked so different and so beautiful. I can also remember the times when I would look through my own eyes at my children and I saw rebellion and suddenly I found myself looking through Father God's eyes and I saw their pain. Once again they all looked so different through God's eyes rather than through my eyes.

THE TREMENDOUS POWER OF GIVING HONOR

The very atmosphere of heaven is saturated with honor. The very atmosphere of hell is filled with dishonor. If we truly want the atmosphere of heaven to fill our houses; then we need to live our life in honor. If we desire our homes to have darkness and oppression, then all we need to do is to dishonor each other. If you honor someone in your heart, it would be impossible to rape or physically abuse them. It requires a heart of dishonor before we can commit sinful acts against others. These two heart attitudes of honour and dishonor will determine how we will treat our fellow men.

> *"What is man, that thou art mindful of him? And the son of man that thou visits him? For thou hast made him a little lower than the angels, and have crowned him with glory and honour. Thou makest him to have dominion over the works of thy hands; thou hast put all things under his feet"*
>
> (Psalm 8:4-6).

God has crowned us with glory and honor. In his sight we have a special value. God paid a high price for us, to reveal what our worth (our value) is. It was the pure, priceless blood of his very Son (see 1 Cor. 6:20). If someone gives me a diamond ring worth 5 million dollars and I throw it into the trash, it still has the value of 5 million dollars. Someone can tell me that my car is worth $5000 and then another person can hand me $1,000,000 for my car. What is the practical value on my car? You may say $5,000, but I will say $1,000,000 because this is the price that someone is willing to pay for it. Likewise, the priceless blood of the Son of God has thoroughly determined the worth of every person, no matter what others might feel or say. It is the value of the blood of Jesus Christ that determines our worth and therefore, we are to honor all men (see 1 Peter 2:17a).

There are many kinds of honor in the Bible. Some of these types of honor are based on character, achievements, age, gender, position, and etc. There is one kind of honor that God requires that we give to all men. This kind of honor does not depend on character, achievement, status, position, age, gender or anything natural. It only depends on one thing. They are an eternal being, made by an eternal Father with an eternal destiny. Three times in the Bible, God is referred to as the

Father of spirits. Every person is a spirit, with a soul that is living in an earthly suit called a body. A heart that wants to honor others will naturally want to bless them. Blessing is the natural outflow coming out of a heart that is full of honor. Pure love sees people in their pain, sufferings, and fears and it yearns to bestow on those hurting individuals great honor to alleviate some of its pain.

> *"So I returned, and considered all the oppressions that are done under the sun: and behold the tears of such as were oppressed, and they had no comforter; and on the side of their oppressors there was power; but they had no comforter."*
>
> (Ecclesiastes 4:1)

Back to my story:

While I was living under the cloud of rejection and my children's behavior looked worse than it actually was. I was feeling the sting of rejection whenever they would disobey me. I understood it as a personal attack on my worth as a man and father. Rejection was speaking to my heart and so I felt even more upset over their disobedience to me. When the heavenly Father started to show me my rejection and how he honored and loved them, my reaction to them started to radically change.

Every parent must understand that while they should discipline rebellious behavior, they should also honor and bless the unique personhood of each child. The identity of the child is not based on their behavior. The true self is the true identity of the individual and it is not the same as their behavior. Their behavior could be all coming out of the nature of the false self that is manifesting in them. Let me explain what I mean.

Isaiah 46:10a says, *"Declaring the end from the beginning"*. God called the end right at the beginning. He does not live in time. He lives in a realm called eternity, where time does not exist. God can see his eternal plan made by an eternal covenant and fulfilled through

His eternal Spirit. Jesus came to a fig tree one day that had no figs, because it was not the time for figs. Jesus cursed the tree and it died, but why did Jesus curse the fig tree since it was not the "time" for figs? The reason he cursed it, was because time was trying to put the Son of God under its power. Jesus is master over time and he will never let time be his master (see Mark 11:13-14). Even so, we are to live in a dimension that does not bow the knee to time. We are to believe we already have what we have asked for (see Mark 11:24). *"Faith is the substance of things hoped for, the evidence of things not seen"* (Hebrews 11:1). In other words, by faith we have what we cannot see and what we are hoping for to manifest, is already made substance through faith. We are also commanded to look at what we do not see (see 2 Corinthians 4:18). In Ecclesiastes 3:15 it says, *"that which hath been is now; and that which is to be hath already been"*. He calls into being the end from the beginning. *"We walk by faith and not by sight"* (2 Corinthians 5:7).

These are amazing Scriptures that reveal a God that is in control of all things and His Word holds everything together now. *"Who being the brightness of his glory, and the express image of his person, and upholding all things by the word of his power"* (Hebrews 1:3). So do I as a father, have faith in God to believe and call my children into being the true self that they were called to be from the foundation of the world in Christ? Or, am I going to identify my children as sin because of their behavior. As a parent we should have the spiritual eyes that Moses's parents did, which enabled them to see their son in the light of his eternal calling. When a child misbehaves, it is so easy to identify them with their sinful behavior, instead of identifying them in the light of eternity; and what the Cross has accomplished on their behalf.

Sin came into the world through one man, but sin is the intruder. The nature and essence of sin is self-exaltation and selfishness. The voice of God calls into being the things that do not exist (see Romans 4:17). So, when we are beholding the nature of sin in our children, will we use the masculine voice which represents the voice of Father God, to call them into being their true self or destroy the potential of the true self? The voice of "dad" is supposed to represent the voice of God. It is the word of God that calls us into being. God's voice said to Gideon who was full of fear, "thou mighty man of courage". God's masculine voice calls the fearful to be bold, and the weak to be strong, and the sinful to be holy. Earthly fathers have a great privilege to represent the voice of God to their families. This is a major role of a godly leader; but there is an evil one that also wants earthly fathers to represent his voice on earth. Fathers have a God given authority to affirm their children and call them into their destiny. This authority is based on their position as a father in the government of God.

> *Will we bind our children into the bondage of self by identifying them with sin or will we see them with the eyes of faith?*

In other words, am I as a father representing God on my child's behalf or representing satan on my child's behalf? Will we bind our children into the bondage of self by identifying them with sin or will we see them with the eyes of faith? The basic meaning of the word bless- is to bless, to kneel down, to cause to prosper, or to praise (Strong's 1288 Barak). When I as a father speak blessing, I am humbling myself in their presence and I am releasing a power from the Lord that is giving them the ability to prosper in life. It is the father that represents God and calls the children into the true self, by affirming them in their manhood or womanhood. What gave Paul the courage to tell the Philippian jailor, *"If you believe on the Lord Jesus, then you and your whole household shall be saved"* (Acts 16:31)? It was the word of faith in Paul's mouth that encouraged the Philippian jailor to bring his family into the kindgdom of God. Am I living under the power of time and submitting to the results of sin in my child or am I living in the Spirit and calling forth the true self; believing that my children will put off the old man with its deceitful lusts and put on the new, true self?

Blessing releases a power from God to call forth that person into their destiny and cursing increases the power of sin in their life.

Proverbs 18:21 says, *"Death and life are in the power of the tongue"*. The apostle Paul did not identify himself with sin; but instead he separated himself from the force of sin and identified himself with the true self. *"For the good that I would I do not; but the evil which I would not, that I do. Now, if I do that I would not, it is no more I that do it, but sin that dwelleth in me"* (Romans 7:19-20). Paul made it very clear that he was not sin, but he was a new creation. *"Therefore if any man be in Christ, he is a new creature: old things are passed away; behold, all things are become new"* (2 Corinthians 5:17).

We need to learn the power of affirmation and blessing as fathers. A father can affirm his child and release blessing into them and call them to come into their purpose and destiny in life. An un-affirmed person has an emotional age that is far below his true age. Without being affirmed, this adult will take on an inner-feeling of immaturity instead of maturity. Therefore, especially if there is a deep emotional or sexual wound from your childhood, you could shut down emotionally. To make this real practical, a thirty year old man that has been physically abused at age nine could still be caring an emotional age of nine years old.

God's way is to have a special time when a child (usually at puberty) is to be blessed to enter into adulthood. At this point in time, this boy or girl should be released into adulthood to be the man or woman that they are meant to be. If a child was never blessed and affirmed then there could be many times in life when trouble or crisis come; when their reaction is a deep inner feeling of being a small child on the inside and incapable of making mature decisions! Sometimes, fits of rage will erupt in an adult because they died emotionally at a very young age and so their emotional age is very young. They might be living in a 50 year old body with a 10 year old emotional maturity on the inside.

We learn from Isaac's reaction when he discovered that he did not bless Esau, the extreme importance of a father's blessing. A person that was not affirmed could feel as if they are living in an emotional prison. It is hard to make mature decisions when you react as a child to your circumstances. Even Jesus had to hear his Father's affirming voice saying, _"my son, whom I love, with whom I am well-pleased"_ (Matthew 3:17). Before Jesus began his official outward ministry he had to be affirmed. How much more do we need this affirming voice to call us into our purpose and destiny, as men and women of God? An adult that has never been affirmed and blessed by his father will grow up feeling like a little child on the inside. This will then produce deep seated feelings of uncertainty and insecurity. Adults that were never blessed and affirmed are usually lonely people on the inside. The longing for father to bless and affirm us creates an emptiness that can only be filled with the blessing and love of a father. This person can go many years and never even know why they have such a pain on the inside. It feels like something is missing, but they have no understanding as to what is that "missing" something? I have personally witnessed thousands of lives be transformed by speaking a blessing over them. Once a person gives me permission to bless them, I simply say "I am just going to give you what your own father should have given you." It is nothing less than miraculous the transformations that I have seen as a result of this one prayer of blessing.

CURSES

Curses are another wound which comes from words spoken by other people (especially parents) or words spoken over ourselves that are negative. We must break agreement with all of these negative words that we ever spoke or received. If we are in agreement with a negative word about ourselves, then we are giving power to it to fulfil the negative impact on our life and circumstances.

DEATH WISHES

A death wish is a vow that we thought or spoke about ourselves. If we wish we were not born or if we do not want to be at a certain place(family, job, school, marriage) this could be a death wish; it is important to break this vow and to declare that, "I want to be whole and I want to live". People think or speak out death wishes without realizing what they are doing. The demonic kingdom wants families to wake up in the morning with a negative feeling about life, work, or lack of work, school, chores, and etc. If a woman has a bad marriage or rebellious children, the evil one will want her to say things or think things that are negative about her circumstances. If a man is out of work, passive, or abused; the enemy desires that he also will think and speak negative and destructive thoughts about life or himself. All of these are death wishes and they open an invisible doorway for the forces of darkness to take away the desire to live and experience joy in life.

Prayer:
"Father, take this child of yours in your arms and hold them."

"Dear reader, I want you to know that every word you speak is important because it comes from you. And every thought is important because it comes from you and you are important. You are not a mistake or an accident and you are not a burden, you're a blessing. You are God's plan and you are important. Come into your adulthood now and come into your destiny. We break all agreement with any death wishes that were ever thought or spoken by you. Father God, release this dear child from all thoughts of death that he/she has ever had. Bring him/her into life and wholeness from this moment on. Amen."

CHAPTER 4
HATRED FOR WEAKNESS AND ITS SYMPTOMS

From the very moment I received the father's blessing from Greg, I was instantly delivered from a spirit of death. From then on over a period of nearly three years I experienced the restoration of my soul and my spirit. Now I know that I am loved. And ever since then I can do things with ease, that before were only possible with the utmost effort. I can participate in life. And this urge to constantly prove myself has left as well. This is so liberating! Thank you Jesus!

– Victoria K, South Germany

This is probably the greatest wound that we witness God heal in the thousands of people that we pray for throughout the nations. Many years ago, I became aware of a certain type of hatred towards women called Misogyny. I have seen this abuse in hundreds of girls and ladies everywhere. After years of ministering, I started to learn about this hatred on a deeper level and it is not just hatred towards woman; it is also hatred towards weakness itself! The woman is the weaker vessel and therefore she will suffer more than a boy or man will suffer. This hatred towards weakness is a specific anger that is directed towards all weaknesses. People that have this kind of hatred are bothered when they see tears because tears are a sign of weakness (so they think). They are also bothered by mistakes in others and in themselves because mistakes are another sign of weakness. When a man has this hatred of weakness (it is more common in men than it is in women) they are usually bound by pornography; and they tend to see woman as a sex object and not as a precious person with feelings and needs. A person that has this hatred will find it nearly impossible to give honor to others, especially women. When a husband has this hatred, there is usually a pattern of this in his ancestral lineage. He can see it in the attitudes of his father and grandfather towards women. Many times when a man runs off with a younger woman, this is the hidden cause that is buried within his heart.

> *After years of ministering, I started to learn about this hatred on a deeper level and it is not just hatred towards woman; it is also hatred towards weakness itself.*

The domestic violence that fills the very atmosphere with coldness is usually due to this form of hatred. When kindness is not present in a family, the entire family might go to church every Sunday, but there will still be this atmosphere of hate in their midst. This kind of hate is most common in the father, but also can be in the mother. Words that hurt, demean, mock others, and lack love are usually coming out of a heart that is full of this hatred towards weakness. A home where this hatred for weakness is present will not have the manifest Presence of God because He resists the proud and this hate always has its root in a proud heart. There are many ways that this form of hate will reveal itself within the context of a family environment. Below are some of the many ways that this can be displayed:

20 WAYS THAT HATRED FOR WEAKNESS CAN BE SEEN WITHIN A FAMILY ENVIRONMENT.

1. Father favors sons above daughters
2. Father tolerates abuse of a brother towards sister
3. Husband disrespects wife in front of children
4. Wife constantly feels that her feelings do not matter

5. Father spends very little time with children and wife
6. Mother is hard towards husband
7. Mother or father scorns their daughter and mocks her
8. An atmosphere that makes visitors feel unwelcome
9. Children are afraid to make a mistake
10. Hard work is more important than a right attitude
11. Father makes fun of his children
12. Either parent uncovers or embarrasses children in public
13. Father does nothing when his son disrespects his mother
14. Seldom will anyone in the family ask for forgiveness
15. Loud talk becomes normal for authority figures in this family
16. Disrespectful behavior is an everyday occurrence
17. Kind words are never heard on mother or father's lips
18. The wife does not desire to have sex with a husband that has hatred for weakness
19. The husband desires sex and is angry at his wife if she does not want to have sex
20. Pornography and adultery are often a part of this relationship

Because of the hardness and the anger towards making mistakes, everyone in the home is careful not to cause the lion to roar. People in the family will probably feel like they are walking on ice. They have to walk very slowly and carefully lest they do something that will make dad angry.

Dr. Margaret Rinck, a Christian clinical Psychologist, has written a book called, *"Christian Men Who Hate Women."* In this book, Dr. Rinck lists characteristics that help women recognize if they are in a misogynistic relationship. Misogyny is a term that basically refers to the hatred of women.

"Misogynists are unable to empathize with their wives' pain and distress. In fact, the pain of their partner seems to enrage them and feed their hatred. Here are some tell-tale signs of a misogynistic relationship. (Rinck,)

1. The man assumes that it is his "God-given right" to control how his wife lives and behaves. Her needs, thoughts, feelings are not considered.

2. He uses God, the Bible, and church teachings to support his right to "tell her what to do", and demands that she submits to his desires, whims, decisions, or plans without question. There is no sense of mutuality or loving consideration. It's always his way, or no way.

3. He believes that a woman's beliefs, opinions, views, feelings, and thoughts are of no real value. He may discredit her opinions in general or specifically because she is a "daughter of Eve and easily deceived". Therefore, her opinions are of little consequence. Or alternatively, he may give lip service to the idea that his wife's opinions count for something, but then discount them one by one because they are not "logical".

4. The woman reports that her husband's behaviour at home is strikingly different from his behaviour at work or at church. At home everyone "walks on eggs" out of fear of displeasing him or setting him off. When the wife points out the difference between his behaviour at home and other places, he is likely to respond, "Oh, quit exaggerating! I'm not like that!"

5. The woman reports that when he is displeased and /or does not get his way, he yells and threatens, or sulks in angry silence. Yet the next day he acts as if "nothing" had happened, and is charming and sweet. No one can predict when he is going to switch from nice to nasty.

6. The woman finds that in her relationship with him, no matter how much she may try to improve, change, "grow in the Word", and etc.; she still feels inadequate, guilty, and somehow off-balance. She never knows what is going to set him off next, and no matter how much she prays, he never changes. She almost feels as if she must be "crazy", and she is sure it is her fault. Even when other relationships at work or school give her positive feedback and encouragement, she loses all her confidence and self-esteem

when she returns home. No matter what she does to change and adapt to his demands, it is never enough. His demands always change and become unreasonable.

7. The husband remains blind to any fault or cruelty on his part. When anything goes wrong in the home or in the marital relationship, the problem is always the *woman*. If she would just be "more submissive" or "be filled with the Spirit" or "obey me like a good Christian wife", everything would be fine. He actually sees himself as virtuous for "putting up" with a woman like her. On the other hand, he can become unreasonably jealous if other people, particularly men, pay too much attention to his wife. Thus, the wife no longer feels free to associate with certain friends, groups, or family members because of her need to keep him happy. Even though these activities or people are important to her, she prefers avoiding them so that she can "keep the peace".

Dr Rinck has divided up misogynistic behaviors into 4 categories:

Type I Misogynist

No physical abuse of his partner. He uses indirect criticism, denies that he is abusive, protestations of love when confronted with his disrespectful behaviour; extremely subtle, and may use flattery to keep woman at his side. Uses logic to control situations. Outargues spouse, totally discounts woman's feelings and thoughts. He rarely loses his temper. He always looks as if he is in control, very reasonable. Out of touch with his own feelings.

Type II Misogynist

Includes Type I behaviors plus more overt verbal tactics such as teasing, bullying, belittling, name-calling, obvious criticism, and unfavourable comparison of partner with other woman. He uses nonverbal tactics such as pouting, the "silent treatment", and dirty looks to show displeasure. May demand special attention. May be jealous of wife's attention to children or other relatives. May use temper tantrum to get his own way. Increase in intensity and frequency of behaviors over Type I.

Type III Misogynist

Uses any of Type I and Type II behaviors plus the threat of physical, emotional, or sexual abuse. More extreme in controlling social life, religious practices, finances, sexual interactions, and matters of daily living. Increase of intensity and frequency of behaviours over Types I and II.

Type IV Misogynist

Uses any of Type I through Type III behaviours plus physical and/or sexual abuse toward wife and possibly children. Level of intensity of abusive behavior is very high and poses a significant danger to the woman. Abusive style has become a deeply ingrained behavior. More extreme in controlling various areas of family life. (Rinck 1990)

This misogynistic behaviour is far too common within typical Christian gatherings and possibly the following quotes could explain why this is so.

"Church father John Chrysostom called women, "whitewashed tombstones", saying that inside they are full of filth, and that marriage was given to men to keep them from submitting to prostitutes". Epiphanius (A.D. 315-403) claimed that "the female was easily seduced, weak and void of understanding. Masculine reasoning will destroy this female folly." Tertullian blamed women for the death of the Son of God. "You are the devil's gateway; you are the unsealer of that forbidden tree; you are the first deserter of the divine law; you are she who persuaded him who the devil was not valiant enough to attack. You destroyed so easily God's image, man. (Parish 1999)

With this kind of prejudice and hatred in the church fathers, it is easy to think that it is acceptable with God. The truth is the heart of God is filled with honor towards the weaker vessels in all of his creation. He has a special love for weakness and He desires to cover, strengthen, and fill these weaker vessels with His love.

........keep reading and let the Father heal your heart.

CHAPTER 5
HATRED OF WEAKNESS AND ITS EFFECTS

I come from Croatia and a lot happened to me during the war. Through the living God I have come into salvation, but complete salvation happened to me only after hearing one sermon of Greg Violi. In Croatia I did the Oujie board at the age of eight and since then I had opened a door to the invisible world. Since then I got catapulted out of my bed every night, and I mean every night and my heart was racing, it was fear upon fear. Many had prayed for me, but freedom only ever came after I listened to the sermon of Greg Violi! Now I have no more nightmares. It has been a year. I do dream a lot about Jesus and about the kingdom of heaven. The sermon was about ungodly soul – ties. I prayed the prayer at the end of the sermon and in the following night I experienced true deliverance. My bed started to shake in the middle of the night and my bedroom was full of light. Suddenly hundreds of strings(ties) were pulled out of me, one after the other. Once all the ties were out, the bed stopped shaking and all the fear left. I was filled with deep gratitude. Just wanted to say thank you. Thank you for preaching with power and thank you for the wonderful works of God.

– Sandra J, Croatia

My wife, Marie and I discover hatred for weakness and its lesser form, misogyny, in every single nation that we have ministered in. The Lamb of God is the Father's supreme Sacrifice and His most precious treasure. Under all hatred for weakness there is a hatred for the Lamb of God. Therefore what God highly values, the devil wants people to greatly devalue. When you have the love of God for weakness, you will be gentle with the needy and kind to the fearful and you will honor all men. Millions of people have grown up in an environment where mistakes were looked down at, simply because it was a sign of weakness. Instead of honoring, affirming, and blessing the weaker vessels, we put hatred and fear of weakness into them.

> *Millions of people have grown up in an environment where mistakes were looked down at, simply because it was a sign of weakness.*

The trauma that results from living under hatred for weakness is felt in 15 areas of the recipient's life.

1. Self-hatred

They feel they are not capable of doing what is required of them. They usually are tormented because they come under a spirit of accusation all the time. This in turn produces a hatred for themselves as a person. If the mother has this hatred for weakness, the daughter will not only hate herself, but will also probably reject her womanhood and attempt to take on male attributes such as: dressing manly, masculine mannerisms, interests and achievements befitting a man, and sometimes even male body parts.

2. Fear

We were made to receive love, if an individual does not receive love, then fear enters in its place. A wife that is receiving hatred of weakness from her partner, might think she is actually receiving love. This can be especially true during times of being charmed by her partner, but this charm lacks true love. This hatred even though outwardly can appear nice, it releases a fear into the one who receives it.

3. Physical Sickness and Infirmities

The body and soul are so interconnected that if the soul is wounded, the body can accumulate different diseases. One such disease that will be a result of this type of hatred is called Fibromyalgia. These individuals have pain in many areas of their body. This is a disease most commonly found in women and it is many times a direct result of feeling uncovered.

4. A Deep Sense of Shame

People that are not honored, but are rather embarrassed by family members will carry shame. Often a father will embarrass his wife and daughter, even in the presence of others. This deep insensitivity is characteristic of this hatred. Many times the one speaking mocking words will not even realize how deeply they just hurt the other person. The more this person receives such treatment, the more they are covered with shame. Jesus was covered with shame, so that we could be covered with honor!

5. Bitterness

The next result of living under this hatred is to hold bitterness in your heart towards the person that is treating you this way. This bitterness will go deeper into their soul. This deep seated bitterness then allows room for these thoughts/emotions, such as: resentment, unforgiveness, revenge, anger, hatred, violence and murder.

6. Unhealed Issues

The person suffering from such unhealed wounds are accumulating these wounds inside of their soul. A visible wound can be seen, but, an inner wound usually needs to be uncovered before it can be healed.

7. Suicidal Thoughts

This dear one will have many thoughts of ending their misery. The thief comes to steal, kill and destroy (John 10:10).

8. Disappointments

Children and wives have many expectations from their father and husband which is their spiritual covering, when these expectations are not fulfilled, deep seated pain, sorrow, and grief begin to enter into their soul. These disappointments will suck the very life out of the person if they are not healed.

9. Depression

The deep wounds that are the result of being disappointed so many times will then cause this person to have deep seated sorrow. They will lack zeal for life and will become depressed.

10. A Spirit of Trauma

A spirit of trauma will cause much abnormal stress and will start to affect the adrenal glands. Adrenal glands are extremely important for healthy living. A spirit of trauma and stress will cause the electrical systems in your body to dysfunction. The abused person will need to forgive the abuser, releasing them from the dishonour and disappointment that they caused. Then they must take authority over the spirit of trauma and stress; commanding its effects to be broken over themselves. Asking the Father himself to release them from all the effects of trauma in their life and cutting off any link that has been connected with the powers of darkness.

11. Addictions

Chocolate, pornography, sex, exercise, and certain drugs all release hormones that give you a good feeling about yourself. Since the abused one has not received the love that he/she needs, he/she could turn to these addictive elements to meet his/her need of love. Another reason we get addicted is because there is an underlying sense of guilt that we have never dealt with. If I have not dealt with all guilt by going to the blood of Jesus and asking for his mercy and forgiveness; I will have more unresolved guilt. This will give me a feeling that I deserve to be punished and this could result in an addictive lifestyle.

12. A Bad Self-Image

Under this harsh treatment by the one person that should be affirming and calling me into being is a very poor self-image. Since this person has not received honor to make them feel good about themselves and their personhood, they then accept a poor self-image.

13. Covenants and Ungodly Soul-ties

This person will start to look for love in all the wrong places. Ungodly soul-ties will probably be established with other needy people. These ungodly-soul ties are a result of this person trying to prove that he/she is special. A young lady may try to prove that she is special by having sexual relations with men. A young man could try to prove he is special by joining a gang. All of these relationships will create ungodly soul-ties with others. After the act of sex, there is now a covenant that will need to be broken between the two, when committed outside of marriage. Once again, we can find all the healing and mercy that we need at the cross through the blood of Jesus Christ.

14. Rejection

Rejection will make this person feel unwanted and uncared for; they will probably try to cover their heart with 3 spiritual walls: rejection, fear of rejection, and self-rejection. This person that has been under the weight of hatred will build these three individual walls to try to cover themselves from any further damage.

15. Uncovered and Unsafe

In this atmosphere of hatred, one will feel uncovered, unsafe, and dishonored. Every day is another day that this person is seeking peace and rest.

Psalm 109:3-16

"They compassed me about also with words of hatred; and fought against me without a cause. For my love they are my adversaries: but I give myself unto prayer. And they have rewarded me evil for good,

and hatred for my love. Set thou a wicked man over him: and let Satan stand at his right hand. When he shall be judged, let him be condemned: and let his prayer become sin. Let his days be few; and let another take his office. Let his children be fatherless and his wife a widow. Let his children be continually vagabonds, and beg: let them seek their bread also out of their desolate places. Let the extortioner catch all that he hath; and let the strangers spoil his labour. Let there be none to extend mercy unto him: neither let there not be any to favour his fatherless children. Let his posterity be cut off; and in the generation following let their name be blotted out. Let the iniquity of his fathers be remembered with the Lord; and let not the sin of his mother be blotted out. Let them be before the Lord continually that he may cut off the memory of them from the earth. Because that he remembered not to shew mercy, but persecuted the poor and needy man, that he might even slay the broken in heart."

There are 15 negative consequences or curses listed in this one psalm. These curses are mentioned in this psalm due to one thing in verse 16, *"because that he remembered not to shew mercy, but persecuted the poor and needy man, that he might even slay the broken in heart"*. These are all curses listed because this individual had hatred of weakness.

Why is this specific form of hate so evil in the eyes of God? First of all, our life is only a vapor of air according to James (see James 4:14). Why do we think that we are strong? We believe this lie, because the liar deceived us into believing that we do not need God's indwelling Presence. Mankind believes that it can make it on its own power, strength, and wisdom. This is one of the results of eating from the forbidden tree, the knowledge of good and evil. A person that has learned to think that he is strong in himself will start to take all of the credit that belongs to God's daily provision of grace. Now, he will boast within his heart about all the achievements that he has made. Within his heart he will start to despise and look down on others; especially if they do not seem to be accomplishing much (according to his standards) in their life. He will also then begin with his thoughts, imaginations, and actions to mistrust his fellow man and family. Then he will dishonor the poor and needy people, accusing them of being so needy and helpless.

> *A person that has learned to think that he is strong in himself will start to take all of the credit that belongs to God's daily provision of grace.*

This attitude of heart is one of the main forces behind dishonor, judging, hardness, criticism, hate, impatience, not caring for others, and abuse. In all truthfulness, just how strong are we? Compare our physical bodies and brains in comparison to the invisible spiritual world. Just how mighty are we against forces of darkness in the invisible, heavenly places? One angel wiped out 185,000 soldiers in the night (see 2 Kings 19:35). David was so strong that he could bend bronze with his bare hands. Fortunately, David understood the importance of being weak; for he said, *"Lord, make me to know my end, and the measure of my days, what it is; that I may know how frail I am"* (Psalm 39:4).

In the next verse David said, *"Behold thou hast made my days as an handbreath; and mine age is as nothing before Thee, verily every man at his best state is altogether vanity. Selah"* (Psalm 39:5). David saw that all men at their very best was vanity. David had to pray that the Lord would let him know how frail he was! Who are the people that abuse and mistreat others; Is it the ones who think that they are strong, or is it the ones that know they are weak? People who know their weakness will probably hardly ever abuse another. The Lord said to his people, *"I will break the pride of your power, and I will make your heaven as iron, and your earth as brass. And your strength shall be spent in vain"* (Leviticus 26:19-20a). God has promised to break the pride of our power or strength. Where I am strong is an area that I am probably lifted up inside of my heart; therefore God will break all my strength so that he can show me my pride. Wherever I am strong for example: if I am a very organized person, then I probably look down at all those people that are disorganized. The pride of my power refers to the areas where I am strong, talented, and good. Those areas in which I have accomplished much are the very areas that will feed my pride. God resists me in every area where I am proud or self-exalted (see Proverbs 16:5, 18:12, 22:4; James 4:6; 1 Peter 5:5b-6; Matthew 23:12). (Note: for more teaching on this subject, see the author's book, "The King's Holy Beauty".)

The original sin that entered the world through Lucifer and then through Adam is: choosing the will of self over the will of God and choosing to be God, instead of being a vessel for God. Self-exaltation is the essence of sin. In self-exaltation, the individual takes the glory for all of his achievements in life. He is self-centred and self is at the very centre of his entire life. *"All we like sheep have gone astray, we have turned everyone to his own way; and the Lord has laid on him the iniquity of us all"*, (Isaiah 53:6). This is the sin that is behind all of the manifestations of evil in the entire world. Sin, therefore is the root and sins are the fruit. Even a Christian that will say he has no sin is deceived and the truth is not in him (see 1 John 1:8). The flesh does not die in me. I, instead must die to it. Romans 13:14 says, *"But put ye on the Lord Jesus Christ, and make not provision for the flesh to fulfil the lusts thereof"*.

What are the lusts of the flesh? Well, the fruit of these lusts are many; but the root is only one and that is to exalt oneself in life! Even with all the evil practices and sins that the people of Sodom and Gomorrah committed, they had only one main problem and it was the pride or self-exalting attitude in their heart.

> *"Behold, this was the iniquity of thy sister Sodom, pride, fullness of bread, and abundance of idleness was in her and in her daughters, neither did she strengthen the hand of the poor and needy, and they were haughty, and committed abominations before me; therefore I took them away as I saw good",*
>
> (Ezekiel 16:49-50).

This Scripture makes it very clear that the main problems of self-exaltation causing one to have fullness of bread is they do not care about the poor and needy people around them without bread. They also have a lot of time to spare, because they use their time only to meet their own selfish needs. It is a haughty, self-exalting attitude on the inside of the heart that releases all kinds of words and actions that are insensitive, hard, hurtful and demeaning to others.

The first sinner that received this attitude called "sin" into his heart was Lucifer. Within his heart were five "I wills" that clearly describe the attitude that this great archangel carried.

> *"For thou hast said in thine heart, I will ascend into heaven, I will exalt my throne above the stars of God; I will sit also upon the mount of the congregation, in the sides of the north; I will ascend above the heights of the clouds; I will be like the Most High God"*
>
> (Isaiah 14:13-14).

Lucifer speaks five I will's within his evil heart and each *"I will"* had a specific meaning behind it.

1. *"I will ascend"*– of my own power and ability, I will climb up in this world. Jesus said I will come down and be as one of them.

2. *"I will exalt my throne above the stars"* – stars represent the other angels. Here Lucifer is saying that he will be the greatest, he will be number one and there will be none greater. Jesus said he will be the least, even to the point of washing the dirty feet of his disciples.

3. *"I will sit also upon the mount of the congregation, in the sides of the north."* This attitude represents a desire to get all the attention. Psalm 48:2 says, *"Beautiful for situation, the joy of the whole earth, is mount Zion, in the sides of the north."* To sit in this place is to put yourself in that exalted place of attention and recognition. Jesus would do a tremendous miracle and then say, do not tell anyone!

4. *"I will ascend above the heights of the clouds"* – This attitude wants to escape the responsibilities down here on earth. This attitude can cause a father to have a baby and then feel absolutely no responsibility for that precious life that God has given him. A mother may ignore her chores at home and her responsibility to care for her precious children. Jesus was a servant to all.

5. *"I will be as the Most High God"* – This attitude requires that others acknowledge you as God. If you do not get the response that you feel you deserve, you will respond in anger. If you do not receive appreciation for all that you have done, you will resent that person. Even being offended when another person disagrees with your opinion. This disagreement could make you very angry. God is never wrong and this attitude wants to be treated as God. Jesus Christ made himself nothing in the eyes of the world. Many times the religious leaders lied and slandered him and he did not defend himself. (For a thorough explanation of the five I will's and the mind of Christ, see the author's book, "Whose Image and Which Mind").

Why is all of this so important? What does this have to do with hatred of weakness? This is the root cause behind the hatred of weakness and it is also the root cause behind all the abuse in the world. For a man to be a true man, godly husband, and godly father; he must understand this truth of the human heart. It is this inner principle of sin in the nature of man that always works through the flesh and it is called the law of sin in our earthly members (see Romans 7:23, 25). We must walk in the Spirit of Christ in order to keep this spiritual law from manifesting in our earthly members.

Hatred of weakness is a deep inner hatred for the heart of the Lamb of God, God's dear Son. If someone has an inner hatred for weakness, they probably greatly dislike humility, gentleness, lowliness, and kindness. God has chosen to display his greatest triumph through a Lamb. He has also chosen to show His greatest power through the gentleness of a Lamb. This is a great mystery in the heart of Father God. Paul called this mystery by different names. Some of the names are **Christ** (Ephesians 3:3-4), **the mystery of Christ** (Colossians 2:2), **Christ in you** (Colossians 1:27), **mystery of His will** (Ephesians 1:9), **manifold wisdom of God** (Ephesians 3:10), **the mystery** (Romans 16:25). Hidden in the heart of the Father is a slain Lamb. Deep within this dimension of the Father's heart called, *"the bosom"*, is a Lamb. When Moses cried to God to show him his glory (see Exodus 33:18), God revealed his heart fully to his servant Moses. He said in response to Moses' plea to see His glory. *"I will make all my goodness pass before thee, and I will proclaim the name of the Lord before thee"*, (Exodus 33:19a). When the Lord caused all of his goodness to pass before Moses, he was manifesting the very essence of his nature to him. In the Scriptures, when name is mentioned, it is almost always a revelation of that one's nature.

Therefore, with each syllable that came forth from the mouth of God, there was also a penetration and saturation of the very essence of that word. For example, when the Lord said, *"The Lord, the Lord God, merciful"* – there was a full manifestation to Moses of the mercy of God. It should not be compared to when a human being speaks a word. Sometimes there might be truth in what they are saying, but there will never be a full revelation and manifestation of that very word. When God spoke each of these words such as; *"merciful"*, *"gracious"*, *"long suffering"*, *"abundant in goodness and truth"*, *"keeping mercy for thousands"*, *"forgiving iniquity and transgressions and sin"*, *"will by no means clear the guilty"*, and *"visiting the iniquity of the fathers on the children"*; he was releasing the full manifestation of all these words to Moses.

One day, the Holy Spirit revealed to me what the Father was showing his servant Moses, it was actually that substance of glory that fills the bosom of God. To say in man's terminology, He was revealing the heart of the Lamb of God to Moses. There is no greater glory that can be seen then the revelation of God's innermost being. This is the very nature of what has been hidden for generations, but is now to be revealed to His saints on earth (see Romans 8: 18-19; Colossians 1:26-27; 2 Thessalonians 1:10, 2 Peter 1:19, Hebrews 1:3). This glory was released from the Son of God on the mount of Transfiguration (see Luke 9:28-32). This is the same glory that God showed Moses. It is the glory of a slain Lamb and one day all creation will behold it together (see Revelation 1:7-8; 5:6; 1 Thessalonians 3:13, Matthew 16:27, and Mark 8:38).

We are called to walk in this realm of glory in Christ and this is how we will reveal the Father that lives in each believer (see Ephasians 4:6). The key to walking in this realm of glory is to love the heart of the Lamb. What I love is what I will be fixed upon. If we love the glory of God, we will fix the eyes of our hearts upon the glorious Lord; by beholding Him, we are being changed from one realm of glory to another (see 2 Corinthians 3:18). This is the secret to allowing the Holy Spirit to change your heart from a heart of stone into a heart of flesh. The entire Bible is a revelation of man's heart. Our translations do injustice to the truth, by trying to explain the spiritual heart by a single definition. The heart is always proceeding out of man. Jesus said *"Out of the heart proceedeth…"* (see Mark 7:21, Matthew 15:19).

Out of the heart constantly proceeds many hidden thoughts that no one except God knows. Throughout the entire Bible, we are constantly confronted with the hidden attitudes of the human heart. For example, many times the Scriptures reveal that the Pharisees would hold a private meeting outside to determine how they might destroy Jesus. None of us would ever have known what was secretly hidden in the Pharisaic heart, unless the Holy Spirit put it into the Bible for us to read. Hundreds of times we read about what someone is thinking on the inside of their heart, because the entire Bible is a revelation of the heart!

One day I was reading about David the boy and I saw that God told the prophet Samuel to go to the house of Jesse and anoint one of his sons (see 1 Samuel 16:1). Then Samuel beheld the firstborn of

Jesse's sons Eliab, and he said, *"Surely, the Lord's anointed is before him"* (see 1 Samuel 16:6b). In other words, this son must be the chosen one by God. Although immediately the Lord corrects Samuel and says to him, *"Look not on his countenance, or on the height of his stature; because I have rejected him; for the Lord seeth not as man seeth; for man looketh on the outward appearance, but the Lord looks on the heart"* (1 Samuel 16:7). After rejecting the first born son, the Lord continues to reject each son that was present in the house. Then Samuel said, *"are here all of thy children?"* Obviously, he perceived that there had to be another son. Jesse's response was, *"well, there's still the youngest and he's with the sheep"* (1 Samuel 16: 11). I particularly like the Prophet Samuel's response, *"fetch him; for we will not sit down until he comes"* (verse 11b). Apparently, Samuel discerned that for whatever reason Jesse chose not to obey the word of the Lord through his prophet. I can picture in my mind all the brothers and their father standing in obedience waiting for the youngest brother to arrive. What happened after David arrived was confusing to me. *"Then Samuel took the horn of oil, and anointed him in the midst of his brethren"*, (verse. 13a). I thought why would God anoint the youngest brother in the midst of everyone? I can recall watching an old movie one day about this scene with Samuel and David, it showed Samuel going out into the wilderness to find him and then he poured the anointing oil over David. I thought to myself, "now, that is the way I would have done it". I would have done it like the movie, all alone with David and in the desert. However this is not how God did it. God poured all that anointing oil over the youngest brother right after all of the older brothers were rejected by God. I thought to myself, God does not want to cause strife or jealousy or problems, does He? God knew the heart attitudes of all the older brothers. Why not just do it the way the movie portrayed it? Almost immediately, I felt prompted to read Matthew chapter 6, when I opened my Bible this is what I read in Matthew 6:1-6.

"Take heed that ye do not your alms before men, to be seen of them: otherwise ye have no reward of your Father which is in heaven.

Therefore when thou doest thine alms, do not sound a trumpet before thee, as the hypocrites do in the synagogues and in the streets, that they may have glory of men. Verily I say unto you, They have their reward. But when thou doest alms, let not thy left hand know what thy right hand doeth: That thine alms may be in secret: and thy Father which seeth in secret himself shall reward thee openly. And when thou prayest, thou shalt not be as the hypocrites are: for they love to pray standing in the synagogues and in the corners of the streets, that they may be seen of men. Verily I say unto you, They have their reward. But thou, when thou prayest, enter into thy closet, and when thou hast shut thy door, pray to thy Father which is in secret; and thy Father which seeth in secret shall reward thee openly."

"Moreover when ye fast, be not, as the hypocrites, of a sad countenance: for they disfigure their faces, that they may appear unto men to fast. Verily I say unto you, They have their reward. But thou, when thou fastest, anoint thine head, and wash thy face; That thou appear not unto men to fast, but unto thy Father which is in secret: and thy Father, which seeth in secret, shall reward thee openly."

Matthew 6:16-18

All of these verses reveal that if I do something to appear in a good way to men, then the secret motive of my heart is to receive honor and recognition for myself. Although if I do something in secret only to be noticed by God; then the secret motive buried in my heart is to please God in all that I do. This secret attitude hidden in the heart is what true worship is all about in the eyes of God (see Colossians 3:23, Luke 16:15). David was always concerned if his thoughts and imaginations would be pleasing in the sight of his God.

"Search me, O God, and know my heart: try me, and know my thoughts: And see if there be any wicked way in me, and lead me in the way everlasting."

(Psalm 139:23-24)

"Let the words of my mouth, and the meditation of my heart, be acceptable in thy sight, O Lord, my strength, and my redeemer."

(Psalm 19:14)

I truly feel that this is why the heart of David pleased the Lord so much.

"And when he had removed him, he raised up unto them David to be their king; to whom also he gave their testimony, and said, I have found David the son of Jesse, a man after mine own heart, which shall fulfil all my will."

(Acts 13:22)

The Lord is raising up the tabernacle of David at this time throughout the world. This tabernacle symbolizes a dwelling place for the Shekinah glory and a place where lovers of God meet with tremendous worship and praise. A place where hearts are enthralled and united as one. Like God said about David that he was a man after my own heart (see Acts 15:16-17). Why did God openly anoint David in front of everyone; even the ones that would be jealous, angry, and hurt? The answer is that God wanted to reward David openly because David's heart did many things that only God knew about and only He could see the motive of love that was in David's heart. At this hour, the Holy Spirit is about to openly reward true worshippers that have been storing treasures in heaven; doing many things for years and seeking only His approval on their lives.

CHAPTER 6

GENTLENESS

I received the father's blessing and now I feel that I am special and loved and somehow complete in a deeper way! I really feel that I am extremely blessed. I want to wash Jesus's feet with my tears.

– Markus, Bavaria

DAVID'S SECRET TO GREATNESS

Psalm 18:35, "Thou hast also given me the shield of thy salvation, and thy right hand hath holden me up, and thy gentleness hath made me

David was a truly amazing man, he had a heart fully devoted to God. He bore suffering and lived uncompromisingly for his Lord and king. He was a tremendous warrior that was determined to pursue all of his enemies until they were destroyed. David won battle after battle. He was an anointed musician that caused demons to flee through his music. He was a great king and true worshipper who invented many heavenly musical instruments for praise. His tabernacle was esteemed by God at the highest level. He was so physically strong that he could bend bronze with his hands. He had such a good attitude that he said, *"Let the righteous smite me, it shall be kindness"* (Psalm 141:5a).

What was the secret ingredient that made him such a great man? He said in Psalm 18 that his secret to greatness was the gentleness of God upon his life. This word for gentleness (Strong's number 6037 anvah) means humility, meekness, and condescension. It is an act of bowing down in the heart. In order to be kind and gentle to the poor and needy, one must come down and condescend to where they are living. Jesus condescended to come to earth as a man. Jesus condescended to little children to reach down and take them into his arms and bless them. The Son of God condescended to women in general (the woman at the well) and the woman in sin (the adulteress). He also condescended to his disciples by kneeling down and washing their feet. Jesus' whole ministry was characterized by a lowly, meek, and condescending attitude of humility. *"Take my yoke upon you, and learn of me; for I am meek and lowly in heart; and you shall find rest unto your souls"* (Matthew 11:29). The lowly, meek heart of the Lamb is the direct opposite of the heart that hates weakness.

The pure love of God will flow through a gentle and a meek heart. Jesus told the story of the Prodigal Son in order to illustrate the heart of the Heavenly Father. This son had tremendously failed his father. He went against his father's wishes, he wasted his entire inheritance, and he dishonored his father's name. In truth, I think it could be stated that this son was a great failure. Although he was a great failure what was the reaction of the father to his child?

- As soon as he saw his son coming a long way off, he started running towards him (Luke 15:20). This meant that his father probably looked as far as he could every day waiting and watching for his prodigal son to return.
- As soon as he saw him a long way off, his heart was full of compassion and he started running.
- His father did not stop running until he reached his son and fell on his neck. This reveals that this father had only one thing on his mind and that was to embrace his repentant, remorseful son.
- He kissed him. This is an outward sign of gentle love.

- He fully restored him, without a single word of reproach. If any father had the legal right to speak harsh stern words of correction, this one did; instead he only revealed his heart of love, gentleness, and compassion to his son.

How many reading this book right now, have ever experienced the gentle compassionate arms of father being wrapped around them after a great failure? How many people have ever felt the fiery lips of love kissing them after they have disappointed dad? How many people ever tasted the goodness of the Lord through their earthly father's actions? Please ask yourself, are you afraid of your father or mother's wrath if you don't do exactly what they want? Are you fearful of their reaction towards you, even when you are really trying to obey? Have you had to live your whole life in fear or did you see the perfect love of God in your father that cast out all fear in you (1 John 4:18).

Were there certain times when you tried to ask for forgiveness from your father; but he interrupted you because he only desired that you be restored and not mention your past failures and sin (see Luke 15:21-22)? Are you still carrying the pain from being punished wrongfully; or rightfully, but with a harsh insensitive voice of your father? When you hear the words of gentleness and kindness, is your mind clouded as to what these words mean? Have you ever tasted gentleness, or are you just hoping that you will not receive another beating? Maybe your greatest wish or prayer is that your father would just be sober when he comes home tonight?

God is love and the main aspect of God's love is purity and unselfishness. There is absolutely no selfish motive in the heart of God towards you. He simply loves you with a compassionate, pure, holy, and unselfish love that burns like fire! Everything that love is, God is. So all that is contained in the Bible describing love is also descriptive of God. 1 Corinthians 13 is famous for being the love chapter of the Bible. This chapter details what love is and it also declares that without this pure love, our entire life is worthless. I believe that you will discover the strongest possible emphasis placed on love in the following scriptures.

"Though I speak with the tongues of men and of angels, and have not love, I am become as sounding brass, or a tingling cymbal. And though I have the gift of prophecy, and understand all mysteries, and all knowledge; and though I have all faith, so that I could remove mountains, but have not love, I am nothing. And though I bestow all my goods to feed the poor, and though I give my body to be burned, and have not love, it profits me nothing,"

1 Corinthians 13:1-3.

Let us look at these three verses of the Bible in depth. Verse one says I can have the voice of angels (this would mean that the world would totally admire the way I speak or sing), but if I don't have the love of God, heaven only hears a lot of noise. Have you ever had a little child just clanging on some noisy toy? How long can your ears tolerate such noise, a few moments maybe? Earth has one standard and heaven has another standard.

In verse two it says I can have the greatest spiritual gift of prophesy and know all mysteries and have all knowledge and even all faith; without God's love I am still nothing. With all these gifts humankind would say I am the most wonderful servant of God. In contrast, heaven says, if I do not have love, I am nothing. Heaven will not even acknowledge me as a person. Heaven considers a person, with the greatest gift of prophecy and faith, without love as nothing.

In verse three it says I can give away all of my goods to feed the poor and I can even offer my body to be burned, but without God's love I am nothing. In other words, a total sacrificial life. A depth of will power that has hardly ever been seen on earth, but if I do not have pure love, heaven says all the outward things that I do will not profit me at all! I personally really needed spiritual understanding with this one. I thought to myself how can I give away all my possessions to feed the poor and needy, and yet still there be a possibility that I do not have the love of God? The Lord said to me that His love is so totally pure that it will never seek anything for itself.

Verse five says that love never seeks its own, love can never be fulfilled by itself. *"does not behave rudely, does not seeks its own..."* (1 Corinthians 13:5) God's pure love is always seeking an outlet in others, for it cannot seek its own. So even if a person sells everything for the poor and they are still seeking for recognition and honor for themselves (this is an extremely high level of human love) it is still not God's love. It is our privilege from God to be a vessel for his pure and holy love. If I give him my body (mind, mouth, hands, feet, eyes, and etc.) to love through me, He will love through me!

Now is the time for everyone that calls themselves by the name of a Christian to become a body for the Son of God to live in and through. The church is called the body of Christ (see 1 Corinthians 6: 19-20; Ephesians 1:22-23). There is a major difference between someone being a vessel for their own personality, ideas, love, and emotions; and that same person instead being a vessel for God's personality, emotions, mind, and love to flow through.

> *The one supreme standard of heaven*
> *is the pure love of Father God.*

The one supreme standard of heaven is the pure love of Father God. The secret to greatness is the gentle, kind, and pure love of Father God. When David said that God's gentleness made him great, he was not comparing the gentle kind, love of God to a soft spoken human temperament or personality. David was saying that God's very gentleness made him the great man that he was. Every parent has the tremendous honor of being a broken vessel for Father God to pour Himself through, in order to make their children great in this life. Divine gentleness creates greatness. Jesus said the least is the greatest. When a child experiences divine gentleness through mother or father, they will also desire to be lowly and gentle and this will bring them into greatness.

Hatred for weakness will destroy all hope of becoming great because it loves the very things that God hates such as: pride, anger, harshness, criticism, and etc. It also hates the very things that God loves such as:

weakness, humility, lowliness, and brokenness. David said that all the sacrifices that the Lord is looking for in a person is a broken and contrite heart (see Psalm 51:17). David was referring to a person that had been deeply dealt with in the areas of his self-sufficiency, stubbornness, and sin. David understood what it meant to grow through suffering, rejection, and betrayal. He also knew these things were designed to afflict him creating within him a clean, pure heart and a clean, right spirit (see Psalm 51:10, Psalm 119: 67, 71). Circumstances will make us bitter or better depending on our reactions. How many fathers as a child have had to suffer under the hand of a dominating, hard parent? They then unknowingly have received a harsh controlling way of dealing with problems like their parents. God's way is that we enter into his rest (see Hebrews 4:1-10) and allow the Holy Spirit to live God's very own life through us. If my life is a constant struggle then which personality is living through me, my own or Christ's? The personality or mind of Christ is full of humility and lowliness (see Matthew 11:28-29, Philippians 2:5-8). Why does there seem to be such a dislike for weakness in our world? Could it be the result of always feeling like we have to be strong in order to make it in this world?

> *Circumstances will make us bitter or better*
> *depending on our reactions.*

I am in total agreement that men especially need strength. The important question is; where does their strength come from? Does our strength come from ourselves or does it come from the source? Jesus said he could do nothing out of Himself (see John 5:19, 30). The perfect Son of God. The God man. The one who was fully God and fully man and never failed or sinned, he said that he could not do one thing out from Himself (actual meaning). Then where did he find his strength from? In Hebrews 9:14 we read, *"Through the eternal Spirit he offered himself without spot to God." "Not by might or by power, but by my Spirit, says the Lord of Hosts",* (Zechariah 4:6). Moses said the Lord is my strength (see Exodus 15:2). Where did the mighty Samson get all of his strength from? The Lord gave it to him and when the Lord took it away, he had no strength. The Holy Spirit exclaimed through Hannah, that, *"by strength shall no man prevail"*, (1 Samuel 2:9). The Lord is actually called The Strength of Israel in 1 Samuel 15:29. David often talked about God being his strength (see 2 Samuel 22:33, 40, 1 Chronicles 16:11, 27, 28; 1 Chronicles 16:2, 29:12, Psalm 8:2, 18: 1, 2, 32, 19:14; 20:6, 21:1, 13; 27:11; 28:7, 8; 29: 1, 11; 31:41, 37:39 and many more).

Elijah had a heavenly angel and he supplied him with enough strength for 40 days (see 1 Kings 19:8). God is so strong that he has ordained strength in babies that is sufficient to stop the enemy entirely (see Psalm 8:2). Isaiah said that in quietness and confidence is our strength (see Isaiah 30:15). This quiet, restful confidence in the Lord will infuse his very strength into us. Paul strongly declared that we are to be strong in the Lord and the power of his might (see Ephesians 6:10). Mankind is so reluctant to embrace their weakness as the soil for the strength of Almighty God, that the Lord may bring us into the valley of Achor as a door of hope (see Hosea 2:14, 15). Achor means troubles. Sometimes, the only way that a person will see their need of God's strength is by coming into trouble. In this trouble, they might come to an end of themselves and begin to see what God always wanted to do in them; which is what they have been trying to do for themselves all along.

If someone has many revelations, it is quite possible they will be given a thorn in their flesh as a messenger of Satan to buffett (beat) them. What the thorn was has no significance or God would have told us. Why the thorn was given is very significant and the Holy Spirit clearly tells us. Paul said a thorn in the flesh was given to him to "keep him from exalting himself above measure!", (2 Corinthians 12:7). This is the self- exalting nature of sin in our flesh that loves attention, to be exalted, lifted up and seen of men (see Galatians 6:3, 12; 2 Corinthians

12:7-10, 1 John 1:8). A thorn in the flesh makes a person feel needy, helpless, dependant, and and poor; and no one wants to have to deal with it. We prefer rather to be healthy, strong, and self-sufficient. Paul cried out to God to deliver him of this thorn, but the Lord wouldn't answer until the third time. Finally, the Lord said no! I think this is a good paraphrase of 2 Corinthians 12:8-9. "My grace is sufficient for you", was the answer. This sure sounds like God's answer was a no to me. I believe the Lord had to deal with Paul's dependency on himself and his own strength. Why did Paul say to the Corinthian believers that he was going to come to them in *"weakness, fear, and in much trembling"* (1 Corinthians 2:3)? Who was Paul afraid of so much, that it even caused him much trembling? Was he afraid of the devil? Absolutely not. Was he afraid of the Corinthian believers? Definitely not! I think they were afraid of him. Was it the fear of God? I do not think he was referring to God at this point. Then who was it? I firmly believe that Paul was afraid of himself. He did not want to hinder the Holy Spirit through his pride, strength, or soul. Remember how Paul told Barnabas that he did not want John Mark to travel with them because he had failed in the past. This doesn't sound like the Father of the prodigal son, does it? Well, Barnabas was of a different breed and so he took Mark with him. Later Paul says to Timothy, Take Mark, and bring him with thee; for he is profitable to me for the ministry.

> *"And some days after Paul said unto Barnabas, Let us go again and visit our brethren in every city where we have preached the word of the Lord, and see how they do. And Barnabas determined to take with them John, whose surname was Mark. But Paul thought not good to take him with them, who departed from them from Pamphylia, and went not with them to the work."*
>
> (Acts 15:36-38)

> *"Only Luke is with me. Take Mark, and bring him with thee: for he is profitable to me for the ministry."*
>
> (2 Timothy 4:11)

I feel Paul was afraid of how he could be too hard and hinder the pure, holy love of God from flowing through him.

PAUL'S TREMENDOUS REVELATION

Paul came to the position where he would rejoice in all of his infirmities and weaknesses because the power and strength of the risen, exalted Christ would now rest and abide on him.

> *"And he said to me, my grace is sufficient for thee, for my strength is made perfect in weakness. Most gladly therefore will I rather glory in my infirmities (weaknesses), that the power of Christ may rest on me. Therefore, I take pleasure in infirmities (weaknesses), in reproaches, in necessities, in persecutions, in distresses, for Christ's sake; for when I am weak, then am I strong."*
>
> (2 Corinthians 12:9-10)

When we believe so much that we can truly rejoice and take pleasure in all of our weaknesses, it is at that point, the power and strength of God can infuse into us and remain upon us. Since, a true man is a person that is God indwelt and God possessed; this man will be living in the strength of another and His gentleness and love is dwelling in this weak broken vessel. This was always the original intent of Father God for his creation. Mankind was never supposed to be a godless, independent selfish creature that believed he could of himself accomplish what needed to be accomplished by God in his life. All of this happened because an intruder called SIN came into the picture. There was a day when I thought all the problems in the world were due to one creature called the devil. But, I read in John 8:34b, "Whoever commits sin is the servant of sin". Jesus is saying that if someone sins, now he becomes a slave to sin. Therefore, sin is the master and the one under its power is the slave. The first slave to sin was the devil. Who is greater, the master or the slave? The master. What is sin? Sin is an entity created by free choice to resist God's rule and to rule in his place. When a creature commits sin, now he becomes enslaved to selfishness and self-exaltation and he cannot get free of this entity called sin. Sin is now his master and he is the slave. Only in Christ Jesus can a person be freed from the tyranny of self-will. In ourselves, we do not have the power to break free of self. Paul said he had the will to do what is right, but he could not find the power in his flesh to do it (see Romans 7:18). Therefore, he discovered a spiritual law, that at the very point he looked to himself to accomplish God's will, the law of sin was activated in him (see Romans 7:21). We actually activate or put into motion the law of sin in our earthly members at the point that we look to our own strength and ability to do good. The only life that pleases the Father is the pure life and love of his dear Son in us. His life is so holy, pure, full of pure motives, and pure love. Our life is so impure, mixed and full of ulterior motives. His pure love is waiting to flow through an empty, clean vessel. God's pure Lamb reveals Father's pure, gentle love. Satan's jealous, proud self is a vessel for sin to manifest through his intense hate for the Lamb.

This is where hatred for weakness has its origin. Like I already said, this is a mystery that is hidden in the very ages of eternity in the bosom of God.

- Power is released in weakness (2 Corinthians 17: 9-10).
- One loses his life in order to find it (1 John 12:24-25).
- Death works in the body, in order to release life into others (2 Corinthians 4:10-12).
- A slain lamb is standing in the midst of the throne of God. (Rev. 5)
- The lame are taking the prey of the strong (Isaiah 33:23a).
- The lowest of men get to rule in the kingdom of The Most High (Daniel 4:17).
- The least are the greatest (Mark 10:41-45)
- Everyone that is high will be brought low (Isaiah 2).
- Everyone that is low will be exalted (Matthew 23:12)
- The beggars are made to sit with rulers and princes (Psalm 113:7-9)
- God chooses the poor, weak, the foolish, the despised as his chosen vessels to reveal his glory and majesty (1 Corinthians 1:27-30).

These are all hidden secrets to the natural eyes of men, but gloriously revealed in the spiritual realm through the key of humility.

> *"At that time Jesus answered and said, I thank thee, O Father, Lord of heaven and earth, because thou hast hid these things from the wise and prudent, and hast revealed them unto babes. Even so, Father: for so it seemed good in thy sight."*
>
> (Matthew 11:25-26).

Self-love replaced pure love and true manhood was substituted by corrupted, sinful manhood. Sin corrupted the nature of man and man became a vessel for sin and forfeited his birth right to be a son and daughter of God. Instead of manifesting the dominion, life and character of father God, man became a slave to sin and under the powers of this dark world.

A Redeemer has come to buy us with his precious blood. Now, we can join ourselves to the Lord and become one with his spirit of love (1 Corinthians 6:17). Now, selfishness will be replaced by unselfishness. And impure, defiled love will be replaced by pure, undefiled love. The hatred for weakness will now be replaced by rejoicing in our weaknesses and affirming others instead of condemning others for their weaknesses. We can now affirm them in their weaknesses. Jesus had to tell his disciples, "Verily I say unto you, except ye be converted and become as little children, ye shall not even enter into the kingdom of heaven" (Matthew 18:3).

No one that hates their weakness will want to become as a little child, but Jesus stated this is a requirement to enter the kingdom of heaven! My dear brothers and sisters, who were the hardest and most abusive people in your life? Was it someone who thought they were weak or someone who thought they were strong?

This topic about hatred for weakness holds the keys to so many problems. For example, if a Christian husband does not show honor to his wife for 2 specific reasons: she is his sister and she is the weaker vessel, then God will cut off his prayer life (see 1 Peter 3:7).

Husbands should demonstrate honor to their wives. This refers to showing the children that mom is very special and this is why I do not make fun of her or her features. Husbands must demonstrate what a royal priest looks like to the family (1 Peter 2:9).

The children should behold dad kissing, honoring and being kind and saying kind words to mom. If a dad is nice to his daughter and harsh and mean to her mother, this will create confusion, anger, and fear in the daughter. She will not understand why dad isn't kind to mom and she will start to resent her father and start making judgments on her father. Those judgments could now start to come back against her when she enters into relationships with men. Hatred for weakness demonstrated toward mom will start to provoke the children to anger. "Provoke not your children to anger, but bring them up in the nurture and admonition of the Lord" (see Ephesians 6:4).

Paul also said, "Be angry and sin not, let not the sun go down on your anger" (Ephesian 4:26). When a father provokes his child to anger, instead of bringing them up in the nurture of Father God, the child will let the sun go down on her anger. Scripture says; be angry, but sin not. What does this mean? Deal with your anger as soon as it manifests in you and then you will not sin and the sun will not go down on your anger. If I get angry and act like I am not angry or stuff it down on the inside, then it will grow into a root of bitterness and it could even take lodging in my conscious mind. At this point, my buried anger starts to create deep frustration in me.

Roots of bitterness, inner vows and judgments start to fill my mind and soul. Life becomes more unbearable and I can start to dream about tomorrow, when everything will be different and better. Tomorrow becomes my new Saviour instead of Jesus and his present grace for me. We need to understand that grace only operates in the present moment. There is only grace for this present moment and not for the future. When we start to think about the future, we are actually stepping outside of the realm of grace that is available for this moment (2 Corinthians 12:9).

> *Roots of bitterness, inner vows and judgments start to fill my mind and soul. Life becomes more unbearable and I can start to dream about tomorrow, when everything will be different and better. Tomorrow becomes my new Savior instead of Jesus and his present grace for me.*

My grace is sufficient, it does not say will be sufficient. It is always present tense. Grace for tomorrow doesn't come until tomorrow, not today. This is one of the ways of the enemy to get us to step outside of grace by influencing our mind to cause us to daydream about tomorrow or to worry about the future. When our mind is focused on the future, we have then stepped outside of the present tense grace of God for us. We are now not abiding in the present sufficiency of God's grace (1 Corinthians 15:9-10). When a father provokes his child to wrath, now his child becomes embittered about his present situation. This then stirs him to look to his future life hoping and trusting it will be better. Unfortunately, he ignores the grace in his present moment and makes an idol out of his future. His future is the false god, (idol) that he starts to trust in, instead of receiving God and his grace now. His future hope causes him to not live in the now. He will start to worry about the future more and more and not appropriate the present grace. Now, the child must repent of idolatry (trusting in the future hope) and start to receive grace for the present. A child that is fathered by hatred for weakness will almost always come under control and manipulation, instead of godly authority. When a child is under control and dominion, they can easily enter into rebellion; which is a normal reaction to a controlling parent.

As children get older, parents should give choices to their children and let them know that there will always be consequences to what they choose. Then the parents must always follow through on what they have said. If children are forced to always do what dad says, they will probably start to resent the control and pressure that is constantly ɪ ιpon them. Rebellion will produce the fruit of control and manipulation in the child and he/she will now start to control others, especially if they have judged their own parents for controlling them. There are 5 main ways that rebellion will manifest in a person's life. Psalm 68:6b says "only the rebellious dwell in a dry, scorched land. If I am living out of rebellion, there is an emptiness and dryness inside of my soul and I probably feel inside like I have no meaning in life.

5 manifestations of rebellion

1. Dishonor – this attitude will be directed towards those in authority over us. This person will not respect the authorities in society, starting with their own parents!
2. Vows – these are thoughts or words spoken; usually out of anger, fear or self-hatred.
3. Anger – if this one has experienced hard, unkind treatment from dad or other authority figures, this person can internalize his anger and it will become self-hatred. Much depression is rooted in disappointments and anger that has turned inward on self.
4. A Stony Heart – this results from bitter root judgments (judgments that we make on authority figures, including God. Thoughts like, "all people in authority try to force me to do what they want. They don't care about me and my feelings!") All judgments will cause little stones to enter the soil of our heart. When judgments are not repented of, the heart will become harder and harder.
5. Defilement – this usually comes from the poisonous tongue of others and self. The tongue is the main tool for defilement.

The heart of Jesus is filled with tenderness, gentleness, honour and compassion. These qualities are never found in the heart of a person with hatred towards weakness. Compassion will freely flow out of a tender heart. Over a hundred years ago, a godly man name G. D. Watson wrote, "Without tenderness of spirit the most intensely righteous, religious life is like the image of God without his beauty and attractiveness. It is possible to be very religious, and persevering in all Christian duties, even be sanctified, and to be a brave defender of holiness, to be mathematically orthodox, and blameless in outward life, and very zealous in good works, and yet to be greatly lacking in tenderness of spirit, that all subduing, all melting love which is the cream of heaven, and which streamed out from the eyes and voice of the blessed Jesus. Many Christians seem loaded with good fruits, but the fruit tastes green, it lacks flavour and October mellowness. There is a touch of vinegar in their sanctity, their very purity has an icy coldness to it." (Watson)

Divine tenderness of spirit has a behavior to it which is superhuman and heavenly. It instinctively avoids wounding the feelings of others by talking unpleasant things and speaking in an argumentative way. Psalm 145:8 says that the Lord is gracious and full of compassion. The literal meaning of compassion is to suffer with. Every believer is called to be full of the Holy Spirit (Ephesians 5:18), therefore we also are to be full of compassion. Do I suffer with others? When I look at my wife and see the wrinkles on her skin, especially near her abdomen, where she has stretch marks from her several pregnancies, what are my thoughts? Do I start to imagine what it would be like if she didn't look the way she does? Instead if she looked like she was 25 year old with tight, smooth, beautiful skin like a young girl, that never had a baby; is this what I imagine? Or do I say in my heart, "Lord thank you for my wife and the pain she bore out of love for me and for our children"? Does my heart fill up with gratitude for a wife that did not even complain while she was in such pain and discomfort for many months?

When the husband comes home from a long, hard day at the job, do I find compassion for the struggles he had to face at his job and do I appreciate his sacrifice so that he could earn money for me and the children? When the husband comes home and sees his wife, do I consider the possibility that she had a very difficult day being with all the children and chores. When I see my children, do I consider how they just seem to irritate me, or do I sense their deep hidden pains, needs, fears, anger and sorrow? Do we see the deep pain, frustration, grief and abuse that so many people carry with them all the time, or am I only conscious of my own needs? If I am only aware of my own needs, I will ask questions like, "Why did he say that to me?" or "I can't believe she did that to me?" or "no one really cares about how I am feeling." Compassion on the inside will prevent us from getting hard on the outside. A compassionate, tender heart is a heart that will affirm, bless and honour others. As a final word to this vitally important chapter, I want to write from a book by Jack Winter.

"Inside each of us is a little child that needs to be loved. When we humble ourselves and admit that truth, then only then, can the Father come and minister His love to us" (Winter, Ferris 1997)

Prayer:
"Heavenly Father, come into all of my wounds that I am carrying, especially the buried memories. Right now, I forgive and release everyone that has disappointed, dishonored or wounded me. I especially release every single person that did not allow me to be real and make mistakes. Father God, I ask that your tender love starts to enter into me and start to heal my fears and self-hatred. Father, show me how valuable I am and how important my life is.

CHAPTER 7

GOD THE FATHER'S ORIGINAL PLAN

For a long time now I have been looking for a home-a place to belong. I felt homeless, without a connection, useless, afraid, and never had a sense of belonging. I was lonely with or without people, needed to fight to find my place, and longed for comfort. I left Germany and felt happy – for a while. Where was this place that would stop all this inner pain? Then I heard Greg online talk about all these things, including the mother and father's blessing. The next time I had a chance I received those blessings from Greg and Marie. I looked into father God's love, and now I could see it and hear it, without distraction. Then I realized, this deep pain was gone! Plus now I am connected to the body of Christ through love! I was brought into the fathers house and I am no longer homeless! "Is not this the fast that I have chosen? to loose the bands of wickedness, to undo the heavy burdens, and to let the oppressed go free, and that ye break every yoke? ....that thou bring the poor that are cast out to thy house?...." Isaiah 58:6-7a KJV

– Kerstin H, Germany

In this chapter we will study Father God's original plan for his creation. First of all, a father loves his children and all that concerns them. God said to Adam, *"Where are you?"* (Genesis 3:9b). The Father wanted to show his heart and his love to his newly created son (see Luke 3:38). He missed Adam's fellowship and companionship. Why was Adam hiding? Something other than God's perfect love had gotten inside of Adam's heart. When sin came into Adam's heart, pure love had to leave. There is no selfishness in pure love. Therefore the self-exalting, self-centred nature of sin took the place of God inside of Adam's heart. Sin corrupted the heart of God's son (Adam) and brought in another plan, another family, and another kingdom.

> *Jesus spoke this way because he knew that only the truth can make us free from the selfishness of sin which imprisons us.*

Jesus said to the religious leaders (people who always fasted, prayed, went to the synagogues, and sung songs to God), *"you do the deeds of your father"* (John 8:41a). Jesus did not ever speak to people in hate. He always spoke in deep, pure love, and truth. Jesus spoke this way because he knew that only the truth can make us free from the selfishness of sin which imprisons us. We can be church goers every week of our entire life and still be in the wrong family and still be allowing the wrong father to influence us. Paul told the Colossians that they have been delivered out of the power of darkness and transferred into the kingdom of God's Son (see Colossians 1:13). There are two kingdoms that are working in the world. Just because a person goes to church, does not mean they are empowered by the kingdom of light. The apostle John made it really clear what the main ingredient is that operates in the kingdom of God.

> *"For this is the message that ye heard from the beginning that we should love one another. Not as Cain, who was of that wicked one, and killed his brother, and why did he kill his brother? Because his own works were evil, and his brother's righteous. Marvel not, my brothers, if the world hates you, we know that we have passed from death to life, because we love the brethren. He that loves not his brother abides in death."*
>
> (1 John 3:11-14)

The pure love of God in our heart is the main way that a person knows that they are living in light and walking in the kingdom of God.

Over 37 years ago, I had a radical experience with the risen Christ. I totally felt that I was a brand new person on the inside. There was peace, joy, happiness, and a deep sense of being washed clean on the inside. The main thing that resulted from this experience was a love for everyone. Even the people I had previously hated, I suddenly now had a love for them. It was as if someone came to live inside of me full of love. I now know it was Jesus Christ in the person of the Holy Spirit (see 1 John 4:13). God's original plan was that his creation would be his family and continually live in his nature of pure love. However, we discover that from the beginning, there was another being in the garden that was controlled by sin. He accuses the Father to his children of deceit, lies, and insensitivity to his children (see Genesis 3:1-7).

Now, the original plan of God needed to be redeemed or restored back to the Father's original purpose! Since there is no time in God, therefore God does not live in time. He planned before man was ever created, that His heart would be fully satisfied with His family.

"Blessed be the God and Father of our Lord Jesus Christ, who hath blessed us with all spiritual blessings in heavenly places in Christ: According as he hath chosen us in him before the foundation of the world, that we should be holy and without blame before him in love: Having predestined us unto the adoption of children by Jesus Christ to himself, according to the good pleasure of his will, to the praise of the glory of his grace, wherein he hath made us accepted in the beloved."

Ephesians 1:3-6

One day, the Son will restore the Kingdom (family) back to Father, so that the Father will be all in all.

"And when all things shall be subdued unto him, then shall the Son also himself be subject unto him that put all things under him, that God may be all in all."

1 Corinthians 15:28

The family of God was defiled by the evil one when he put a thought into the mind of Cain to kill his brother (see 1 John 3:12; Genesis 3:11). The evil one will use sin because he is one with his master (sin) and sin is also his very nature. The choice will always be mine to make, will I choose my will (sin) or God's will (love). Will I deny myself and choose God's unselfish love or will I choose my selfishness and deny my Creator? (see Luke 9:23). A person can be a born again Christian and still choose to serve selfishness and allow sin to be their master. This is a clear teaching of Romans chapter six and Romans chapter 12:1-2; which teaches us that we are to present our bodies, dead to sin and alive to God, as a living sacrifice. The fire of love will consume the sacrifices and the world will behold that good, holy, and perfect will of Father God.

> *Father God will say to us just like he said to Cain, "If you do well, your countenance will be lifted up, but if you don't do well, your face will look downcast and sin's desire is for you, but you must master sin" (Genesis 4:6-7).*

In Christ, there is divine power to stand united with him and consider your innermost being as dead to sin and alive unto God (see Romans 6:10-11, 16, 19; 1 Corinthians 6:17, 19, 20, 1 Corinthians 1:30; Hebrews 13:20-21; Colossians 3:3-5; 2 Corinthians 10:4-5). The person that has not joined themselves to the risen Christ is considered to be in Adam. The person united to Christ is considered in Christ (2 Corinthians 5:17; 6:17). Both Adam and Christ are actually spiritual dimensions in which we are all living. In the dimension called "in Adam", there is the spiritual law of sin and death; and both of these spiritual laws govern this realm/dimension. In Christ there is the law of the Spirit and the law of life and there is a supernatural life in this realm/dimension that comes through the Holy Spirit. It is called Zoe life or the very life of God (see 1 Corinthians 15:22, Romans 7:23, 7: 47-49; 8:2; 1 John 5:12)

Self-sufficiency is not a good thing. It will block a person from entering into the Father's original plan of making his Son be the all-sufficient One for his creation. But this wicked false ruler called the evil prince, continues to speak to our pride that "you don't need God, you can do it all by yourself".

The apostle Paul told the Corinthian believers that no flesh will ever boast or glory in the presence of God. The Father has placed us in his Son and he made his very Son to be all that we will ever need.

> *"But of him are ye in Christ Jesus, who of God is made unto us wisdom, and righteousness, and sanctification and redemption, so that according as it is written, He that glories, let him glory in the Lord!"*
>
> (1 Corinthians 1.29-31).

This is the very meaning behind God's name I Am. He is all that we need to fulfil all that he desires and that which will totally satisfy us forever! The liar would have people, especially men, believe that it is a negative thing being just a vessel for Christ, receiving all that we need from Christ. Within the new creation or new humanity, there is a life that is perfect, complete, and whole in every way; and this perfect life is Christ Himself.

> *"And have put on the new man, which is renewed in knowledge after the image of him that created him; where there is neither Greek or Jew, circumcision nor uncircumcision, Barbarian, Scythian, bond nor free; but Christ is all and in all"*
>
> (Colossians 3:10-11).

The life is in His blood and in us who are the new creation in Christ. It is His blood that is flowing through each part and member. Through this blood of the eternal covenant, God's very life is working into us everything that is needed to be pleasing in his sight.

"Now the God of peace, that brought again from the dead our Lord Jesus, that great Shepherd of the sheep, through the blood of the everlasting covenant, make you perfect in every good work to do his will, working in you that which is well pleasing in his sight, through Jesus Christ to whom be glory forever and ever"

(Hebrews 13:20-21).

The Redeemer has come and He has poured out of His Spirit upon all flesh. Not by power or by might, but by my Spirit says the Lord of Hosts (see Acts 2:32-33; Zechariah 4:6). In the body of Christ, called the Church, there is life flowing through every spiritual cell and the essence of that life is pure heavenly love. This is why it is so crucial that I deny self in order to be his disciple. One of the very first things that I knew God spoke to me was, "If you truly want to be my disciple, you must deny yourself".

"So likewise, whosoever of you that forsakes not all that he has, he cannot be my disciple", (Luke 14:33). Jesus is saying that in order to be a true disciple of his we must forsake all that we have. We must have absolutely no trust or confidence in anything that comes from our self (the natural realm).

> *The original plan was for God to have a family of sons and daughters full of his very image; increasing and multiplying his very image throughout the earth*

We need a supply from a heavenly realm that comes out of a heavenly treasure full of an abundance of every good thing! The original plan was for God to have a family of sons and daughters full of his very image; increasing and multiplying his very image throughout the earth. The very DNA of God was put into Adam and he was in the image and likeness of God. After sin entered the world, another DNA was superimposed over the original DNA, and Adam had a son in his own image (Genesis 5:3). Everything that a lover of God goes through has one major purpose, which is to restore the exact image of the Son of God to the Father's creation.

"And we know that all things work together for good to them that love God, to them who are called according to his purpose. For whom he did foreknow, he also did predestinate to be conformed to the image of his Son, that he might be the firstborn among many brethren"

(Romans 8: 28, 29).

It grieved the Son that the world did not know his Father and he yearns for the Father's love for his children to fill the entire church.

"O righteous Father, the world hath not known thee; but I have known thee, and these have known that thou hast sent me. And I have declared to them thy name, and will declare it; that the love wherewith thou hast loved me may be in them and I in them"

(John 17:25, 26).

Everything has its source and origin in Father God and everything is trying to be restored to its origin. God will have a people that are filled with His Presence. The Son glorifies the Father and the Spirit comes into our hearts with a cry saying, "Abba, Father" (see John 17:4, Romans 8:15; Galatians 4:6). At the end of time, Jesus, the Son will turn everything back to the Father as if to say "here Father, here is your family the way they were always meant to be".

"Then cometh the end, when he shall have delivered up the kingdom to God, even the Father; when he shall have put down all rule and all authority and power."

1 Corinthians 15:24

"And when all things shall be subdued unto him, then shall the Son also himself be subject unto him that put all things under him that God may be all in all."

1 Corinthians 15:28

Paul had to even beg the Christians in Corinth to be reconciled to God (see 2 Corinthians 5:20). They were believers, so why was Paul saying to them to be reconciled to God? Theologically, they were already reconciled. I believe, Paul was encouraging and beseeching them to be reconciled back to the Father. There are many born again believers that are fearful of receiving the pure love and acceptance Father God has for them. There are many reservations in the hearts of many Christians toward the Father.

Many families lack the purity of love and instead joke, belittle, and ridicule one another. No child should grow up in this kind of atmosphere. These attitudes which release ridicule and joking which defiles a child, will always leave defilement in the heart of the child. *"Unto the pure all things are pure; but to them that are defiled is nothing pure; but even their mind and conscience is defiled"* (Titus1:15). When Father God comes with His pure love to this person, he has great difficulty to receive it; because he is unable to see its purity. Therefore, many children expect this kind of treatment from the world and from God. The evil one has harmed, defiled, abandoned, and rejected many children through an earthly father. Therefore they are fearful of how their heavenly father will treat them.

If you feel that God is far off, then you need to be reconciled (brought back) into his pure, loving arms. One of the ways that Jesus tried to restore the original plan of being a family for God was to call his grown up, strong adult men, "children" (Mark 10:24, John 12:36, John 13:33, John 21:5). Can you imagine; mature tough men like the disciples, being referred to as children by a person about their same age? When you are looking through the Father's eyes, you will only see your brothers and sisters. Paul also seemed to like this word "children". (see 2 Corinthians 6:13, Galatians 4:19, Ephesians 5:1, 8; 1 Thessalonians 2:11; 1 Thessalonians 5:5) Peter also used the word children (see1 Peter 1:14). John also liked this way of a addressing the Christians (see 1 John 2:1, 18, 28; 3:7, 19; 4:4; 5:21; 3 John 4).

There was a certain man named Saul and he had a specific hate and it was directed to a group of people called Christians. One day, God came to Ananias and told him to go and see Saul. Ananias obeys the voice of God. As soon as Ananias enters the home where this ex-murderer and hater of Christians was staying, his first word to Saul was to say, "brother" (see Acts 9:17). Saul shares what happened to him with Ananias, and he later tells other believers that Ananias called him brother (see Acts 22:13). When a person is looking through the Father's eyes, he will only see brothers and sisters. The family is being restored and fulfilled according to God's original plan.

Closing Prayer:

"Father God I pray for the person reading this book right now. If he/she grew up in a defiling atmosphere and therefore their conscience is defiled. Father I ask that you come upon him/her now and cleanse him/her from defilement. Pour into each one a sense of value and honor; and may he/she never look upon themselves again as a joke or unimportant."

CHAPTER 8

SPIRITUAL FATHERS

As the oldest of five kids I grew up with a dad working two jobs and a lot of tension in the house. My parents did their best but I was deeply starved emotionally. I had no self-esteem and an eating disorder, always looking to people to give me stability. When I married at age 23 and had three kids, this hole in my heart did not go away and my marriage was almost over. I cried out to God. He sent me a born-again believer and I came into four months of intensive closeness to Jesus Christ. I got baptized and devoured the Bible, the Church I attended was legalistic and a deep hunger stayed with me. Then, after 20 years God opened a door for me to come to a seminar with pastor Greg. At the end of the seminar I wanted prayer but was so blocked I could not ask. Greg came up to me and asked about my relationship to my Dad. He started praying and leading me through prayer and then he spoke the Father's Blessing; speaking all the wonderful words I longed for ever since I was a child! Since then my deepest longings are at peace. I feel I belong, I feel protected, and I am carried. It is actually a dramatic change; I never felt like this in my entire life! I have come home!

– Jaqueline Bruhn-Rois - (Korfu), Greece

Spiritual fathers are called to reveal the heavenly Father to his children. Paul said there were many teachers, but not many fathers (see 1 Corinthians 4:15). Today, there is a tremendous need for spiritual fathers and mothers in Christ.

Let us investigate how the spiritual father Paul treated his spiritual sons. Paul called Timothy: "my son"), "my own son, and "dearly beloved son" (1 Timothy 1:18, 2 Timothy 1:2, 2 Timothy 1:2).

"To Timothy, my dearly beloved son: Grace, mercy, and peace, from God the Father and Christ Jesus our Lord. I thank God, whom I serve from my forefathers with pure conscience, that without ceasing I have remembrance of thee in my prayers night and day; Greatly desiring to see thee, being mindful of thy tears, that I may be filled with joy",

2 Timothy 1:2-4.

Paul longed to be with Timothy because he remembered Timothy's tears. These would have been tears of affection, love, and sorrow because they had to be separated. Paul told the Thessalonians that he treated them like a nursing mother with her baby. He also told them that they were so dear to him that he longed for them. Paul referred to Titus as mine own son (see Titus 1:4). Paul called Onesimus, "my own son". Spiritual fathers will affirm, bless, and honor their children. So many people just want someone to encourage, hug and kiss them, and to say something simple like, "I love you" or "you are special".

"A father of the fatherless, and a judge (and protector) of the widows, is God in his holy habitation. God makes a home for the lonely; he leads the prisoners into prosperity. Only the stubborn and rebellious dwell in a parched place. ",

Psalm 68: 5-6 (Amp).

God is such a great father that He is Daddy in the depths of his holiness and he has a great concern for anyone that is without a man, such as a widow or an orphan. Jesus told his disciples that *"he will not leave them orphans"*, (see John 14:18). Father God does not want anyone to be alone or lonely. In the very beginning of creation, one of the first words that we have recorded that God spoke was, *"It is not good for man to be alone"* (Genesis 2:18). God does not desire that one single person be alone. He puts the lonely into a family. Now, this is where the church must see their responsibility to be the family of God for mankind.

> *Many Christians come to church every week and they are smiling on the outside, but they are lonely on the inside.*

Many Christians come to church every week and they are smiling on the outside, but they are lonely on the inside. Loneliness is a major cause of premature death and many physical diseases. Millions of people have been abandoned, wounded, ignored, or abused by their earthly families. I believe this is a major reason that we are now seeing more killings, violence, confusion, and more suicides than ever. What is the family that God the Father is putting all these lonely souls into? It has to be his, own special family!

Maybe you have been spiritually abused by a leader in the church that should have revealed the Father God to you.

The more you love someone, the more you are risking being hurt by this same person. If someone walks down the street and says something mean to you, but you do not even know who they are, then this remark will probably not even affect you. Although if you really appreciate and love someone, and they say something hurtful or mean to you, this could deeply wound you.

The purpose of God has always been that everyone who calls themselves a Christian would be full of the love of Christ. Within the churches, there should be these types of love:
- **"storge"** love (motherly love),
- **"agape"** love (divine, self-less love),
- **"phileo"** love (brotherly, and sisterly love),
- **"eros"** love (sexual intimate, passionate love between married couples

These four types of loves should be flowing profusely in each local body of believers worldwide. By this love will all nations know that we are truly his disciples. This is why it is so vitally important for spiritual fathers and mothers to be a spiritual covering of love in the church; instead of allowing sin to dominate, divide, and destroy. The love of spiritual parents should cover the effects of sin within the family of God. Proverbs 10:12 (Amp) says, *"Hatred stirs up strife, but love covers and overwhelms all transgressions (forgiving and overlooking another's faults)."* 1 Peter 4:8 (Amp) says, *"Above all, have fervent and unfailing love for one another, because love covers a multitude of sins (It overlooks unkindness and unselfishly seeks the best for others)."* All kinds of wounded people will come into a church gathering seeking to find healing and restoration. These people in the context of the Father's family that is full of his love, will find wholeness.

ELIJAH SENT TO RESTORE FATHERS

"Behold, I will send you Elijah the prophet before the coming of the great and dreadful day of the Lord; and he shall turn the heart of the fathers to the children, and the heart of the children to their fathers, lest I come and smite the earth with a curse"

(Malachi 4:5-6).

Does this sound a bit odd or strange? I could think of many people that could be a possible candidate to restore fathers into the family of God, others such as: Moses, John the Beloved, Abraham; but not Elijah!

What an amazing portion of Scripture! Father God is going to send Elijah to turn the hearts of the fathers. Beloved, the heart is the problem and it is the cause of all the hate, pride, abuse and lack of love in fathers. Their hearts must change.

The heavenly Father is not an old man with a long beard sitting on a throne in which he has to be careful that he doesn't mistakenly fall off because of his age. I wonder how many of us picture God the Father as an old looking person? I believe the Father is eternally young and has eternal strength and power. He is not this old looking person that is

always nice. I read in Romans 11:22a that I am to *"behold the g
and severity of God"*. As Paul persuaded men, we also are to know ___
terror of the Lord , *"Knowing therefore the terror of the Lord, we persuade
men"* (2 Corinthians 5:11a).

> *It is the pure, loving rebuke, and chastening of God
> that produces the fruit of repentance that leads to life.*

The true love of God will come at times with rebuke and chastening
(Revelation 3:19). It is the pure, loving rebuke and chastening of God
that produces the fruit of repentance that leads to life. A spiritual father
called Paul said that godly sorrow works repentance that brings us into
life. Paul was not glad that the Corinthians were made sorrowful; but
he was thankful that their sorrow led them to repent because it is in
repentance that we find life (see 2 Corinthians 7:8-10). True spiritual
fathers will know when to speak a rebuke and when to be quiet. The
spirit of Elijah is a true fathering spirit that will be clothed with the very
strength, glory, truth, and love of God. The beloved Apostle John said,
it brought him the greatest joy, to hear that his spiritual children were
walking in truth, (see 3 John 4). I must say that there must be much
breaking, cleansing, and purifying before one can truly reveal the pure
love of the Father to others. Many years ago, I could speak truth to
anyone. It is easy to speak truth. It is not so easy to speak truth always
in love. There were many times that the Holy Spirit would rebuke
me for disciplining my children in anger. Every time that I revealed
anger to my children in times of correction, I had to humble myself
and ask them to forgive me for my anger, then I had to be faithful
in godly discipline. Disciplining in anger always grieves the Father's
lowly heart. We earthly fathers must reveal the heavenly Father's
heart to others, especially in times of correction. How many men or
women of God have ever heard their father (natural or spiritual), call
them son or daughter? Why is it so hard for so many godly people
to call one another by their titles: son, daughter, child, beloved one,
or etc.?

> *I must say that there must be much breaking, cleansing,*
> *and purifying before one can truly reveal the pure love*
> *of the Father to others*

I think it is so hard because there is a war against father and fatherhood in the world. It was the reproach of the Father that the son carried to the cross of Golgotha. *"Because for Thy sake I have borne reproach; shame hath covered my face." "Reproach hath broken my heart"* (Psalm 69:7, 20a). Anyone that truly desires to be a spiritual father, burning with the fire of pure love, will also be in a war that is against fatherhood. Six times in the Bible we are commanded to greet one another with a holy kiss. If ever there was a need in the world for spiritual fathers to greet their children with holy kisses, today is that time. When God says the same thing twice, it is real important, but when He says the same thing six times, I think we better do it.

Spiritual fathers should have 12 main qualifications within their heart.

1. A man who fears God
2. A real desire to be a vessel for God the Father to live through. A willing vessel for a Consuming Fire (see Isaiah 33:14b, Hebrews 12:29, Song of Solomon 8:6; 1 John 4:9). Our God is a consuming fire and in the center of that fire is the purest, most unselfish love imaginable.
3. Someone that has received years of training under another godly authority, and who has learned the importance of submission (see Hebrews 13:17, Ephesians 5:21, 1 Thessalonians 5:12-13).
4. Someone that knows Him who was from the Beginning. *"In the beginning was the Word and He was with God and He was God"*, (John 1:1). To know the second person of the Godhead and to have a deep love for the truth. His Word is truth and Jesus said he was The Truth. (see 1 John 2:13; 1 John 5:7)
5. Walking in the love of God on a daily basis. (see 1 John 2:6-11)
6. Someone that lives the gospel, especially at home (see Titus 1:16).

7. An affectionate, caring compassionate man toward the poor and needy (see 1 Thessalonians 2:7-8).

8. No hatred for weakness. A main qualification for a man to be a Priest is that he is compassionate with the ignorant and the one's gone astray, because he himself has so much weakness (see Hebrews 5:2).

9. A man that lives in the atmosphere of honor and he gives great value to each person (see 1 Peter 2:17a, 1 Timothy 6:1-4).

10. No fear of man. Not living to please people, but instead living his life to please God. (see 1 John 4:18a)

11. A man that walks humbly with his God and reveals wisdom that is from above in his daily walk (see James 3:13-18).

12. A man that knows the vital necessity of denying self in order to reveal Christ (see Luke 9:23).

If these 12 heart attitudes are in a man, he will be prepared to be a tremendous spiritual father. One of the reasons that there is such a great need for spiritual fathers is because there are so many spiritual orphans. Many children of God appear normal on the outside, but are feeling like an orphan on the inside. An orphan will always feel as though they must earn their way through life, constantly seeking someone to adopt them into their family and accept them.

For many years as an anointed man of God, I lived in my false self. The false self is the hurt, wounded little boy that is constantly trying to feel capable of withstanding adulthood, with all of its major trials and responsibilities. The false self often reacts out of anger, fear, or pressure. The problem is that the false self always seeks to find its identity in what it does and how much it possesses. This false self will always give in to people it considers "important" because deep in its mind, it is not important. An orphan mind-set is so easy for the false self to receive. Many people receive a lie when they are very young. This lie tells them that they do not deserve to be living; they must prove it. This creates great stress in the mid-section of their back and they will struggle to prove they deserve to be living. The true self knows its identity is in Him alone (see Acts 17:28). The true self can stand in Him and see the salvation of the Lord in every situation. The true self can face disappointments with calmness and boldness. The true self is the new person that has become one in spirit with Christ. The good news is that there is complete healing for the person who is 50 years-old and feels like a little boy or girl that is waiting for adoption.

Right now, receive this prayer for yourself if you are a tense, stressful person.

Prayer:
"In the name of Jesus Christ, I pronounce you free from this lie and I break its power over your mind. Every thought and every word that you have is important because it comes from you and you are important. You are not a mistake. You are not an accident and you are not a burden. You are a blessing. I now command all stress to go out of your body; especially stress in the lower back, in Jesus' name!"

A kind word from a spiritual father can do so much to change a person's life. I think the following story will reveal this. (Please forgive the one unwholesome word!)

***

Fred Craddock and his wife loved to get out of the city and visit Gatlinburg, Tennessee, whenever possible. They often dined at an Alpine-styled restaurant in the village, choosing their favorite corner table in the candlelit romantic atmosphere. Fred narrates a true story of the time when he and his wife were dining there late one afternoon. Too late for lunch and too early for the dinner crowd, they had the whole restaurant to themselves. Their intimate meal was suddenly interrupted by a flood of light flowing from the open door as a large, lumbering hulk of a man burst into the café. Looking around, he spied Fred and his wife and promptly pulled a chair up to their table and interrupted their date.

"Hi, I'm Ben. So, you folks come here often?" he abruptly asked them.

Agitated and annoyed, Dr. Craddock fished for words that could convey to the intruder how unwelcome his presence was. With an unfriendly tone and pronounced scowl, Fred responded, "We like this private, cozy nook. We come here to enjoy one another."

"So, you're from out of town", the burly local exclaimed, "where ya'll from?" Pushing back from the table, Dr. Craddock eyed the unwelcomed guest with a stern stare that had frightened many a seminary student. "Yes, I am from Atlanta. "What is your work there?" quickly asked the intense intruder.

"I am a professor of homiletics", replied Dr. Craddock with his deepest and most holy voice, hoping again to repel the man. Undaunted, the stranger retorted, "Ah, a preacher are you. Now, I've got a good preacher story for you". Dr. Craddock frowned and his wife sighed, both to no avail. The stranger continued....

"I grew up in these parts just a few miles down the road in a small town with a one-room schoolhouse, one store, and one church. My mother was a woman of the streets, if you know what I mean, and most nights various men from hereabouts could be seen coming and going. I had a problem... Not with my mother but with my father... Truth was, I didn't know who my old man was. From the time I could talk just about, I would ask mother, "Who is my father?" to which she would reply, "Son, I simply don't know." She refused to discuss the matter beyond that simple answer. "The guys at school during recess would tease me about not having a father. I was the only one in school without a dad. Mocking me, they would call me, 'Ben, the Bastard Boy'. Sorry about that, but it's the truth. And so everyone at school called me that and I lived daily with the shame of not knowing my real father. One week when I was about ten, the local church was holding their annual revival. Now, mother and I didn't go to church. It was for respectable people if you know what I mean. We just didn't fit in with her activity. I felt like an orphan filled with shame. I thought my real father should at least claim his boy; but those were the thoughts of a child who didn't know then that my real father probably had no idea I was his boy. "

"So, anyway, where was I? Oh, I know", Craddock and his wife were now caught up in the story and had forgotten being offended with the stranger. Ben continued his tale. "The revival. So, this meeting with a guest preacher was going on in town and everyone was going to it, pretty much, except mother and me. Business was slow for her during revival week. And I was curious. Didn't know what a revival was except for the words, "REVIVAL THIS WEEK." printed in large red letters on a white banner strung up between the two oaks by the road in front of the church. Anyway, the second night of the meeting, I heard such shouting and singing coming out of that little church that I wanted to get closer and hear it. So, I snuck into the back of the church and spied out what they were doing. It seemed fun enough so I stayed and listened to the preacher too. He shouted a lot but what he had to say about the Bible and Jesus and God was interesting enough. So, I returned each night in the middle of the singing and sat in the back so no one who knew me would see me. And, each night right before the end when the preacher had everyone close their eyes and bow their heads for a prayer, I snuck back out. I thought no one even noticed I was there. On Saturday night, the last night of the revival, the singing went longer and so did the preaching and I began to doze off. Didn't notice when the preacher started praying and so I was a little late in moving out the back door. Suddenly, a loud booming voice stopped me in my tracks. "Young man, going out the back door", shouted the preacher. "Stop"! And before I could run, I felt his hand on my shoulder as he stood right behind me. I slowly turned around and looked up at what I expected to be an angry, scowling face. To my surprise, the preacher had kneeled down to my level and his expression was kind and loving. In a soft voice the preacher asked, "Son, what's your name?"

"I paused just a moment and then had an idea. If I said in church what the kids had named me on the playground, then he would be so shocked that he would let me go and I would run out, never to come back into that church again. I was frightened, but his tender look kept me glued to the floor. Slowly I spoke the dreaded words, "The other kids call me, 'Ben the Bastard Boy'". "That so", mused the preacher in a soft, thoughtful tone. After a moment, a sparkle seemed to come to his eyes and he responded, "I know your father..." I immediately interrupted him, "O Sir, if you could only tell me who my daddy is. All my life I've wanted to know. My mother doesn't know. No one does. I've been without a father all of my life." "Wait a minute. I know who you are. The family resemblance is unmistakable. You are a child of God!" With that he patted me on the back and added. "That's quite an inheritance, son. Go and claim it!" Dr. Fred Craddock knew he had heard one of the best preacher stories ever. Smiling, he reached out to shake Ben's hand but before he could do just that, the large Tennessee native wheeled around and started to leave. "So, preacher, and madam, that one statement literally changed my life."

He explained that his name was Ben Hooper (1870-1957) and that he had become a lawyer and had been elected to two consecutive terms (1911-1915) as a governor of the state of Tennessee. He had led a responsible and respected life made possible by a person who cared enough to encourage a little boy to know his real Father. Stunned and amazed, Fred and his wife marveled at the divine appointment they had just experienced. (Holloran)

The orphan will probably have a very difficult time talking to his Heavenly Father. Although Jesus said, when you pray say, "Father"! Jesus made it very clear in several of his teachings that we do not need to go to him. Instead we can go straight to the Father, because the Father loves us (see John 16:26-27).

May you be totally set free from the orphan mind-set and live as an actual child of the Emperor and King of all Kings!

CHAPTER 9

THE UNAFFIRMED, HURTING LITTLE CHILD IN AN ADULT'S BODY

I was invited to have dinner with Greg Violi. After dinner I was talking with Greg about my relationship with my father. Later that evening Greg spoke a father's blessing over me. About two weeks later, a fellow student immediately came towards me and told me that I had changed. I asked what she meant with that and she said that I have become mature and manly, and that I was not insecure anymore. In that moment I understood the power that is in the father's blessing.

– Alexander K, Germany

So often a child has expectations of people and are often disappointed because their expectations are not fulfilled. Therefore a person is often carrying inside of themselves deep painful disappointments from their childhood. It is important that they learn to forgive others for the disappointments they caused in them and forgiving them for the emotional pain they felt when they were disappointed. One is forgiveness for the action and the other is releasing them for their attitude which allowed it. Many people grow up in an atmosphere of dishonor, but they do not realize that they have been dishonored. The original plan of Father God is that we give honor to one another. To receive honor makes an individual feel special and valuable; not receiving honor makes an individual feel worthless. Many will have forgiven people for what they did to them, but they have never released them for the way they made them feel. When an individual has been degraded and dishonored by another person, that person could carry deep shame and pain inside. In Psalm 139:24, David says, *"See if there be any wicked way in me, and lead me in the way everlasting"*.

> *If we hold on to the disappointments of the past;*
> *then we will be cheated from living in the love, power,*
> *and joy of the present.*

The word David uses for wicked means pain and sorrow. So much of our evil reactions are coming out of our deep pain and sorrow. I have personally witnessed people coming into the Father's love, releasing those people that disappointed and dishonored them and then received major healing in their hearts. I have seen wrinkles disappear instantly. Many people look about 7-10 years younger within a day after joy and gladness returns to them. It is a beautiful sight to behold God pouring His love into a broken heart. Broken-hearted people need to know the Father. Jesus described the Father as never breaking a bruised reed, (see Matthew 12:20a). If we hold on to the disappointments of the past; then we will be cheated from living in the love, power, and joy of the present.

Many people that I have prayed with suffered from deep emotional pain stemming from their childhood. Usually it involves embarrassment, shame, fear, and some other form of abuse. During times of prayer ministry, these people have experienced renewed hope, a changed perspective, and healing in their soul and body. These great disappointments will fill a person with things such as: depression, passivity, grief, sorrow, and death. The good news is that the pure love of God is so strong that it drives out most of the aforementioned conditions in five minutes.

After prayer, many times these individuals now have to relearn how to live. In the past they were used to living in the false self, carrying deep seated disappointments, and a bitterness in their spirit. They are now free from these past diseased feelings. These spirits of bitterness must leave when love comes in, afterwards they feel light, free, and happy. This is so new for many people that they are now uncertain about how to live without all that baggage they used to carry.

Saul represents ruling in the power of the flesh and David represents ruling in the power of the Spirit. *"Therefore they inquired of Jehovah further, will the man yet come hither. Behold he has hid himself among the baggage,"* 1 Samuel 10:22 (Darby translation). Will we be as Saul and hide among our baggage and stuff? Or will we be as David and leave the baggage with the keeper of the baggage, *"And David left the things he was carrying in the hand of the keeper of the baggage, and ran into the ranks and came and saluted his brethren"*? (1 Samuel 17:22). When you get rid of your baggage, you can now face the enemy and be prepared to take your true self and fight in the battle.

I prayed with thousands of men that were deeply bound by a spirit of passivity. Usually, this spirit enters at an early age after the boy has experienced shame and fear. He will then try to hide his feelings and start to control his environment as he gets older to cover up his shame and fear. His pride will prevent him from admitting his great need of help and now passivity starts to gain a foothold inside of him. This man must release every one that made him afraid and ashamed and totally break agreement with all passivity in his generational line and in himself. From this moment on, he can now make appropriate choices in life.

If a man was deeply wounded at a young age, such as 7 year old, he could just shut down emotionally. This would mean that as he continues to grow physically and mentally, even spiritually; he may stop maturing emotionally. He could be a 35 year old man who is living as a 7 year old boy emotionally on the inside.

It is dad's role to affirm his children and to call them forth into their adulthood and destiny. The glory of children is their father. Dad is the splendor and jewels that his children carry with them, wherever they go. If a father never affirmed his son, but instead beat him, screamed at him and belittled him, this boy could grow up carrying this ashamed, fearful, little boy on the inside.

Proverbs 17:6 says that the crown that a grandfather wears, are their grandchildren. In other words, what gives majesty and splendor to a grandfather are the seeds borne by his children. Life is a tremendous gift from God and it should never be taken lightly by anyone. We see a grandfather in the Bible called Jacob who immediately wants to bless his grandchildren as soon as he sees them. He clearly understood how important blessing them was, and I think we could say he wanted to keep his crown polished (see Genesis 48:8-9).

Pro 17:6
Children's children are the crown of old men; and the glory of children are their fathers.

1. Glory - beauty, splendour, glory

1. beauty, finery (of garments, jewels)
2. glory
   1 of rank, renown
   2 as attribute of God
3. honour (or nation Israel)
4. glorying, boasting (of individual)

Fathers are what children possess to show their splendor, beauty like a young girl who is wearing her shiny, beautiful jewels and she is very proud of those beautiful, gorgeous jewels that she is wearing.

The crowns of grandfathers are their grandchildren, but the glory of children is their fathers. God has placed majesty and splendor in the family unit. If a family will see how valuable each member is, there will be a visible demonstration of love between them.

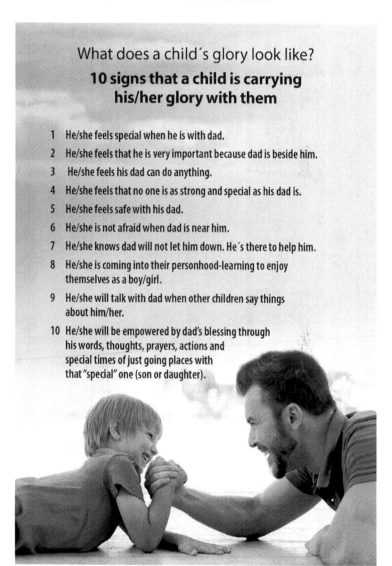

What does a child's glory look like?
10 signs that a child is carrying his/her glory with them

1 He/she feels special when he is with dad.

2 He/she feels that he is very important because dad is beside him.

3 He/she feels his dad can do anything.

4 He/she feels that no one is as strong and special as his dad is.

5 He/she feels safe with his dad.

6 He/she is not afraid when dad is near him.

7 He/she knows dad will not let him down. He's there to help him.

8 He/she is coming into their personhood-learning to enjoy themselves as a boy/girl.

9 He/she will talk with dad when other children say things about him/her.

10 He/she will be empowered by dad's blessing through his words, thoughts, prayers, actions and special times of just going places with that "special" one (son or daughter).

This diagram shows two girls with different outward appearances. Sometimes, parents can dress their children very nice outwardly, but inwardly they feel as if they are an orphan. They have poverty in their soul, but prestige in their appearance.

Which picture would best illustrate you in your childhood?

A small girl with a filthy, dirty torn old dilapidated dress holding a dirty little blanket in her hand

or

A small girl wearing a beautiful, brand new dress and a bracelet that is shining gold and a necklace that is shining gold and two large earrings that are both shining gold.

Which one of these pictures represents you on the inside while you were growing up?

My dear reader, have you ever felt like you are prince or a princess? Or have you always felt like a pauper? Please forgive your father for every way that he dishonored you and did not affirm you. Release him entirely and ask Father God to pour His glory and love into the depths of your innermost being.

Prayer:

"Father, right now I release my father (mother) from the pain, disappointments and emptiness that I felt growing up. I ask that you release me, God, for all the times I said negative things about myself and my life. I break every death wish I ever made and I declare that I want to live and be whole from this moment on."

Growing up should be a special time with many good memories. The home environment should be one of the safest places that a person can think of. When thinking about the first 16 years of your life, what is the mental image that comes to your mind when you read the following words? Is it an image of being covered and safe, or is it an image of being uncovered and unsafe?

Mental images connected to important aspects of life
- Father – God's agent to cover the family
- Mother – God's nurturing agent to comfort the children
- Discipline – God's method for training children in His ways which are meant to bless them
- Reproof – One of most necessary parts of learning and receiving wisdom (see Prov. 1:23).
- School – Another important and necessary avenue of learning
- Home environment – God's ordained place for all growth
- Sex – a very sacred and beautiful thing that God created for procreation and pleasure

- Church – God's very life dwells there and it is meant to be the soil for life to grow
- Work – should be an interesting place and should bring satisfaction
- Christian fellowship – God's ordained ways to experience love from the Father
- Siblings – should bring gladness to your heart
- Neighborhood – should be a place of fun, respect, and sense of community
- Friends – people that you are free to share and love together
- Church Events – should never be a burden, but instead they should be fun activities filled with joy and love.
- Leaders – you should feel safe with, protected, and special in their presence
- Being with people of the opposite sex – should be enjoyable, fulfilling, easy and productive.
- Being together with older people – you should create an atmosphere of respect, honor, and appreciation in your heart
- Being with people who are younger – should give you a sense of love and joy
- Being alone – should make you feel now it is time to rest and be quiet
- Being together with your spouse – this should bring deep satisfaction because the one complements and fulfils the other

All of these words and phrases should give a mental image of being covered, being at peace, feeling safe, and feeling free to enjoy life.

> *If these words immediately relay a mental image of being unsafe and uncovered, then you are probably in real need of deep healing.*

Since God puts the lonely into families, (see Psalm 68:6) He has a family to plant you into so that complete restoration can take place in your life. God knows our every need and he is determined to provide all that a loving powerful and caring father should provide for his children. The ideal place that is in the heart of Father God is the place "the family of God", or what is commonly referred to as "Church" today. This supposed to be a place of safety, love, healing, honor, and friendships where all feel accepted and special. So much of the inner wounds from our past is due to abuse, dishonor, and abandonment, the provided place of healing is God's family. Sometimes, a person will start to pity their self and they feel anger towards God for allowing their circumstances.

Now, rebellion may grip this person's heart. The Lord will provide an environment that they desperately need; but because of the deception of self-pity, this person cannot see that the Lord has provided a place for them to find their healing. This person will now dwell in a parched and dry land, even though a family is ready and waiting for them. *"God sets the solitary in families; he brings out those which are bound with chains; but the rebellious dwell in a dry land"*, (Psalm 68:6). Self-pity often is the result of a child being left alone and abused. This precious child has no one to turn to, so they turn to self-pity. I have watched God heal husbands through prayer, then secretly a spirit of self-pity works in the wife to destroy all that the Lord began in her husband. Self-pity will torment the mind, stir up rebellion in self and others, criticize, and make others feel that they are the guilty ones. Many ladies that feel like they are losing their mind have a spirit of self-pity that is hiding. Self-pity will start to hate the very ones that can help this needy person. Usually someone that is bound by self-pity has been abandoned by many people. They must choose to forgive and release each person that has abused or abandoned them; without forgiving and releasing they will stay in a dry, parched land with deep seated anger. Self-pity, rebellion, and bitterness will make an individual feel that they do not need anyone. Although the truth is that they desperately need a loving, godly family that Father God can use to bring healing, refreshing, and freedom to their soul.

Some Characteristics of Unaffirmed Men:

1. Emotional immaturity that will manifest as laughter when talking to others at all the wrong moments. (ex: serious talk and a sudden outburst of laughter)
2. Fear in relationships
3. Self-hatred
4. Fear of taking on leadership roles; even if they are called and chosen by God to be a leader.
5. A childish feeling deep inside at times of crisis.
6. There may be addictions with the hope that "I will feel good about myself".
7. Jealousy along with rejection. When others are honored this thought of rejection will speak to them.
8. Being upset if they are not acknowledged, when someone else is acknowledged.
9. No sense of self-worth. This person does not see himself as a king and priest (This is discussed in a later chapter).
10. Deep seated anger towards people that threaten them, like King Saul's anger towards David.
11. A major dislike for pressure from others.
12. A deep empty void in their soul that they keep trying to fill in many different ways.
13. A fear of making mistakes and a constant struggle to do better and to do more.
14. These men tend to be stressful and tense individuals.
15. A very constant, deep aching that never seems to go away.

In an article about 20 years ago in Sports Illustrated magazine, Bo Jackson, the famous professional baseball and football player made an enlightening comment. "My father has never seen me play professional baseball or football. I tried to have a relationship with him, gave him my number, said, "Dad call me, I'll fly you in. Can you imagine? I'm Bo Jackson one of the so called premier athletes in this country, and I'm sitting in the locker room and envying every one of my teammates whose dad would come in and talk with them after the game" (Sports Illustrated 1995).

One would think that someone that is as nationally famous as Bo Jackson would not have needed his father to affirm him. With the entire nation saying how great he is, why did he still need to hear his dad say it? Because, this is how God made us. Fathers are the glory of their children and not the media or the world. Is it not amazing that God has put such a high honor on a father that his child is really only desperately seeking his approval and not the approval of the world. This is why many people who are famous in the world are not really happy. Bo Jackson, I believe, would be a good example of this truth. Fathers have the honor and privilege by Father God to call his child into manhood/womanhood and to cover them with his love. Many beautiful people also will find some fault with the way they look.

Unaffirmed men usually sense a deep shame inside of them, because they did not have the covering and approval of the one they yearned to receive it from. In the Bible, we see a man that also did not have his father's affirmation and his name was Jacob. He told the most important man on earth, Pharaoh, "The years of my pilgrimage are a hundred and thirty, few and unpleasant have been the years of my life" (Gen. 47:8,9a).

Why did Jacob say his life has been few and unpleasant? Jacob's father had a favorite son and his name was Esau. Jacob was the one person that God specifically said "Jacob have I loved" Malachi 1:2.

Some Characteristics Of Unaffirmed Women:
1. Rejection (including self-rejection)
2. Self-Hatred
3. Self-Pity
4. Sexual promiscuity (in an attempt to prove their womanhood and get love from a man)
5. Lots of inner fears such as: fear of not being accepted, fear of failure, not being good enough, and fear of not being protected.

6. Pain in the lower back, due mainly to trying to overcome the lie that says you do not deserve to be living, you have to prove it.
7. No sense of self-worth.
8. Hatred of their own womanhood, sometimes wishing to be the opposite sex.
9. Suicidal thoughts
10. Panic attacks
11. Tremendous difficulty trying to connect with God.
12. Death wish.
13. A sense of never fitting in or belonging.
14. A deep anxiety about most things that you attempt to accomplish.
15. A problem with overeating (trying to compensate for the horrible feelings that you have on the inside).
16. A deep ache on the inside, but never knowing why it is there.

A father should never show favoritism to his children because the other children will have jealousy, envy and hate, including self-hatred into their hearts. Now is the hour for all unaffirmed men to come inside the fire of father God's own heart and find your healing.

***

Hyyng Ho picked me up at the airport. "I have two daughters," he said. The younger one, Kyung Hee, is in her freshman year at university and is doing very well in her studies. As a family we are all very proud of her. The older one, Soon Hee, is still living at home and helps us in the store." I knew this dad loved both of his daughters, but I couldn't help but sense some disappointment in his voice as he talked about Soon Hee. After the seminar Hyung Ho came to me and said: "Jack, I never realized until I heard you speak this morning how much I had missed as a child, growing up in a home where I did not know the love of a father. I guess you could say I was a survivor. My own father died in the Korean War shortly after I was born. "This afternoon as we prayed, I wept. The pain in my heart was so deep. I don't think I have ever cried like that in my entire life. "As you were holding me in your arms, like a father would hold his small son, I realized how good it felt to be embraced. For so long my heart has been empty, crying out for a kind of love that neither my wife nor my daughters could ever give. "Jack, I still need a dad. How wonderful it is to know that God is my Father! As His child I can rest secure in the knowledge that He loves and cares for me, with no strings attached." I'm not the same man who picked you up at the airport. I'm different, changed in a way that is hard for me to put into words." "Now I want to go home and be a father to my own daughters. Never having known the embrace of a loving father, I realized that I, too, have failed my family. I have never hugged my own children, even when they were very, very, small." When the seminar was over Hyung HO went back to the city. Determined to keep his promise to the Lord, he immediately walked into the family store, took Soon Hee in his arms, and gave her the biggest bear hug a father could ever give a daughter. Surprised, but pleased, Soon Hee wept, then smiled, right in front of the customers she had be waiting on! "I didn't care," said Hyung Ho, "what people thought. It felt so good to love my daughter and be free enough to show it. "Now my heart is overflowing with love for my family, my God, and for others. It is truly a miracle. For the first time in my life I know I am loved. I know that God is my Father!" (Winter, Ferris 1997)

***

So once again, I feel to repeat as a concluding thought for this chapter the words of Jack Winter from his book, "Homecoming". "Inside each of us is the little child that needs to be loved, when we humble ourselves and accept that truth, then and only then can the Father come and minister His love to us."

Fathers, it is time that we affirm our sons and daughters, preventing them from going to others to seek affirmation; when deep down, they really just want "dad" to give the affirmation! There is a river of pure love that is flowing from the Father heart of God and as parents, we have the privilege of tapping into this river of love and affirming our children and speaking life and blessing into their inner beings. Fathers have such a great honor and power and authority that God has bestowed upon them. Every father can choose to be a channel to release hugs, words of kindness, encouragement and hope in a world that so often seems without hope. Affirmation comes in many ways. Whatever a father does or says to reveal to his child that he or she can fulfill the whole purpose that God intended for them will affirm them in life and this will help them to find their true self in Christ.

Prayer:
Father God, shine your light deep into my memories and reveal any hidden offense that has not been healed and forgiven yet. Any hatred towards anyone that has abused me or anger towards life in general. I now let it go. I choose not to have any hate or anger in my heart from this moment on. Thank you Father!

CHAPTER 10
FATHER'S LOVE OR SATAN'S SELFISHNESS

When I heard Pastor Greg talk about the Father and Mothers blessing and half the church went to the front of the Church for prayer, I did not go to have anyone pray it over me. Instead, I prayed that my parents would be open to give me such a blessing and speak it over me. It took me a month to muster up the courage to tell them about it. Although I could only explain the principle to them in part, we spoke these blessings over one another in our family as good as we could. We stumbled through it, but in the end it brought us closer. The change occurred slowly, but I can see that we understand each other better, that we are more open to one another and that we are able to pray together. It has deepened our relationship as a family.

– Nadja H, Germany

Imagine a multi-billionaire, who is a genius, invents the most incredible super-computer. No other computer has ever compared to this one. This one has 750 billion mainframes that are all linked. It is very complicated, and it has a super advanced circuitry system. Just the building required to hold this computer is made out of glass and 100 stories high and equivalent to the size of Texas.

Everyone who beholds this computer can only stand and stare. The inventor created this computer with the intention that every person that used it correctly, would advance their natural abilities 20 times more than their average. All of the user systems such as: physical, emotional, neurological, spiritual, intellectual, and etc. would all be far advanced than normal. As the world is beholding this invention, an evil villain is planning how he could destroy this super-computer.

This evil villain invents a special virus that he found could access and corrupt the computer. While the entire world was beholding the most magnificent creation ever, this villain was polluting it with his virus. One unfortunate day the computer starts to malfunction. The inventor was mystified as to how this could have happened. It was discovered that the machine had a virus and it took many months searching for some kind of solution. Finally, the genius invented a serum that he could put inside the computer so that it could cleanse it entirely from the effects of the virus. Within a few weeks from the administration of the serum, the computer was clean from all its defects.

This story has great significance. First of all, the computer is the description of the marvelous Creator's invention of the human brain. Secondly, if it is operated according to the plan of its Maker, the result will be fullness of life in every way. Thirdly, the virus that was introduced is sin. Fourthly, the villain is the evil one that is referred to as the prince of this world (see Eph. 2:2). Lastly, the serum to solve the problem of the virus is the blood of Jesus Christ. *"Let us draw near with a true heart in full assurance of faith, having our hearts sprinkled from an evil conscience, and our bodies washed with the pure water",* (Hebrews 10:22). God made the brain in the most phenomenal way. There are neurochemicals that give people a good feeling about themselves. They alleviate stress and give them an overall sense of well-being. These valuable neurochemicals are activated in the brain when a person experiences warm, caring hugs and embraces. Affectionate strokes send strong affirming messages to a person that they are special and valuable. The warmth of a mother's and father's embrace stimulates the release of these all-important feel good chemicals.

A young child has little reasoning ability, but an older child and teenager are capable of much more ability in making clear decisions.

Paul in his writings (1Cor. 13:11) talks about the difference between a child's reasoning and an adult's reasoning. As Paul Hegstrom notes, "the young child learns by boundaries, directives and either positive consequences for obedience or negative consequences for disobedience". (Hegstrom 2006)

David said that God made him fearfully and wonderfully (see Psalm 139). Conscious choices to change will start to create new neurological wiring in our brain. With childhood abuse and traumatic experiences, the pathways are formed in which our thoughts travel on. These neurological pathways are very important because they set the stage for how we will probably react to certain problems that we face in life. Negative experiences will affect our organs negatively.

This is why we must form new neurological pathways through thinking godly and wholesome thoughts; thus the importance of renewing our minds and thinking on that which is good. Choice is a vital part of coming to complete healing within a person's life. We have the God given power of choice; whereby we can decide to love, no matter how bad the memories. The choice to love will then create new pathways in the brain and the Holy Spirit (by our faith) will infuse His love into our minds and this will create new pathways in which our thoughts will travel and they will fill our organs with health and life.

> *The virus of sin (self-will) will always pollute and corrupt the computer (person) and so the choice to reckon one dead to sin and alive to God in Christ Jesus must be a constant ongoing attitude of heart (see Rom. 6:11).*

Sin is my will choosing to do my selfish thought against the unselfish thought of God. The nature of sin is to choose the will of the creature instead of the will of its Creator. Each thought has a central focus and it is either selfishness or unselfishness. Love is purely unselfish and has the good of others in mind, although selfishness has only its own good in mind. Self-will, in opposition to the divine will, is the very essence of sin. To choose to love is a major aspect within the healing of a father or mother wound. The virus of sin (self-will) will always pollute and corrupt the computer (person) and so the choice to reckon one dead to sin and alive to God in Christ Jesus must be a constant ongoing attitude of heart (see Rom. 6:11).

The tense of the verb reckon, in Romans 6:11 is present imperative, which is a command to constantly consider this to be. Therefore, what we are to do is to continually trust the fact that I am in union with Christ, and are dead to all selfishness and alive to God. This is a choice of my heart, and this attitude becomes my true desire. The Holy Spirit will come into my faith to work his life and desire into my heart. I am not depending on any feeling or action, but I am standing firmly on an established fact in the spirit. In Christ, I am dead to sin (self-will). This is not a promise that we are to believe in, but it is a fact that we are to live in! Once again choosing to love un-selfishly is a crucial decision that will precede this truth from manifesting in my heart and life.

So, what is the end of the story? There is no end. We either will walk in the full life of the creature that God has made by being cleansed and filled with His mercy and love; or we continue to be dysfunctional in our behavior. As we live in our dysfunctional behavior, we are either allowing the virus of sin to rule in us or to rule over us through the abuse from others.

Dear brother and sister, please draw near to God with a true heart in full assurance of faith in the power of his blood and be cleansed from all the defilement that sin has caused in you.

THE MANIFESTATION OF SIN IN MEN

What is the main fruit of sin in a man? The main way that sin will manifest in men is a selfish lifestyle. This man's life will reveal the nature of sin as a self-centered attitude within his mind and actions.

The choice that these men make involves "their" feelings, "their" needs, and "their" desires being satisfied, while their family suffers. A father is the head of the family. The head is where the source of leadership is found, a covering for the body, and has the main task of making decisions for the family. The body cannot function without its head it must always be present or available for his family. Lastly, the head is the very source where life flows from in order to reach the other members of the body. A family with an absent father is like a soldier that has been decapitated in the middle of the battlefield. Life can be compared to a battlefield, especially in today's world with hatred abounding. The father gives strength, covering, and stability to his wife and all the children. He has the God ordained calling and fortitude to enable him to accomplish all that the family needs. A man, so to speak, is fitted for the job of a leader within the family. Although if father is not present, the family will literally feel like a soldier in the middle of a war decapitated.

Fatherless epidemic from **National Center for Fathering**
- 20 million children are living in a fatherless home in US
- Fatherless families are 44% more likely to raise children living in poverty
- 90% of all homeless and runaway children are fatherless
- 10% more likely to abuse chemical substances
- 71% of all adolescent substance abusers come from a fatherless home
- 80% of adolescents in psychiatric hospitals come from fatherless homes
- Fatherless children are twice as likely to commit suicide
- Fatherless children experience more accidents and have a higher rate of chronic asthma, headaches, and speech defects
- 9 times more likely to drop out of school
- Less likely to attain academic and professional qualifications in adulthood
- Fatherless children are more likely to score lower than the norm in reading and math
- 70% of adolescents in correctional facilities come from fatherless homes
- 60% of rapists were raised in fatherless homes

- 11 times more likely to have violent behavior
- 20 times more likely to be incarcerated
- 9 times more likely to be raped or sexually abused in a home without a biological father
- 70% of teen pregnancies are in fatherless homes

(National Center for Fathering)

There is no stage in life that a person does not need and desire loving, kind, strong arms to embrace them and say "I love you". About 80-85% of everyone in church on Sunday morning has never had their earthly father say to them "I love you" while growing up. Even if a person is filled with hate and murder, underneath all that hatred is a little child that is longing to be loved. We were born for love. God is love and it was always his intention to reveal the deepest longing of his paternal heart to his children.

***

Following a seminar in Ontario, a woman shared this powerful testimony concerning a baby's need for love.

"Down through the years my husband and I have been foster parents to ten children. To touch these little ones with the love of Christ has been a life-changing experience. But as we look back, one little guy in particular stands out.

Stephen had been born into a very troubled family that had wanted a baby girl. In fact, the parents had told the brother and sister that, should the baby be a boy instead of a girl, they were to have nothing to do with 'it'.

So, fed with a propped-up bottle, Stephen was rarely held or spoken to, spending most of his time lying flat on his back in his tiny wooden crib. As he grew, bottles of lukewarm milk and fruit juice were placed at the end of his bed for him to pick up and feed himself at mealtimes or whenever he was hungry.

When the authorities became aware of the situation, all three of the children were removed from the home and placed in foster care. It was decided that Stephen, now 13 months old, would be placed in a home separate from his siblings because of the original rejection.

When my husband and I went to meet Stephen for the very first time, our hearts went out to this little one. A chubby ball, his eyes were big and brown, but seemingly unresponsive. His head, which was totally out of proportion to the rest of his body, was flat on the back. Stephen was unable to sit up, even when assisted. Having gone for over a year with so little stimulation, he seemed locked into a world of his own, oblivious to the sounds and movements around him.

Stephen had been tested for infantile autism and epilepsy. He had also undergone an EEG. We were told that he would not develop much beyond a small a child in terms of overall mentality and that he would demand a lot of our time. Were we willing, were we able, to take on such a challenge?

Why, yes! Of course. There had never been any question in our minds. From that very first moment in the nursery we had known that Stephen was coming home with us!

Everything took time. But as we poured ourselves into this little guy, he soaked up all the love his heart could hold. Each day my husband and I could see some evidence of change.

At first Stephen would not cuddle and resisted any effort on my part to hold him close. Then, as he began to bond with us and trust that we would care for him, he slowly gained control over his body and the world around him. From lying on the floor to being propped up beside my husband, he began to pull himself up and crawl. Now he not only noticed objects that were placed in front of him, but he also began to propel himself across the floor on all fours to retrieve a lost truck or a favorite teddy bear.

Stephen's first words, which he had heard us say over and over again, were 'I wuv oo'. What an encouragement for the hearts of a mom and dad who had trusted God for a miracle!

For years my husband and I had been unable to have a child of our own, so Stephen was an answer to prayer. I had wanted a little boy with big brown eyes, and God, knowing the desire of my heart, had delivered!

About nine months after Stephen was placed in our home, the social worker came to visit. Shocked by what she saw, she could not believe that this was the same little guy that had been so unresponsive in the nursery. He was delightful, full of life and running all over the place!

'How did you do it?' she asked. 'What brought about these changes?'

'We talked to him' I said. 'We sang with him. We prayed for him. We just loved him!'

A straight 'A' student, Stephen is now in high school. He plays the trombone and loves computers. When he completes his schooling, he wants to serve the Lord as a missionary in Africa." (Winter, Ferris 1997)

***

The original plan of God was that He would have an intimate close love relationship with his family. He loved his children and as soon as Adam was hiding from "daddy", his heavenly Father said "Adam where are you?" (see Genesis 3:9b). Pure love never seeks its own. Since God's pure love never seeks its own, then it has to give it away to others. The love of God is always seeking to pour itself out on others, since it cannot be completed or satisfied in itself. *"If we love one another, God dwells in us, and his love is perfected [fulfilled] in us."* (1 John 4:12b)

Sin came into the creation through Lucifer choosing his own will over the will of his maker. Then sin came into the world through one man, Adam and mankind became an instrument for his own selfish will and desires instead of the desires of God. Now both the devil and man have the same nature, which is sin. All children are born with the same sinful nature. This nature is self-centered, self-absorbed, independent, and only concerned about its own needs.

When sin came into man, he became independent and consumed with selfish love instead of pure love. C.S. Lewis' definition of the original state of man is one in which the sinless creature, would be perfectly and utterly selfless. He also says the soul is but "a hallow" that God fills. This creations union with God is almost by definition, a continual self-abandonment and opening, an unveiling or a surrender of itself. To clarify what Lewis is trying to describe is to say that the original creation was made a selfless, empty container, who in union with its Creator, would be utterly filled with His life and wholly abandoned to His divine will! Strictly speaking, a soul that is in union with the heart of God would be utterly self-abandoned to the will and purpose of God. A selfish soul would abandon God and others in order to glorify its own selfish wants and desires. This selfish love will abandon others to meet its own needs. A selfless soul will abandon its own selfish desires in order to meet the needs of others.

A major consequence of the fall of man in the garden is a stubborn self-exalted way of looking at others. This self-centeredness causes a father to not be there for his children. When did abandonment start? It started with Adam abandoning his Father God (see Luke 3:38). God did not abandon Adam; it was the creation that abandoned the Creator. God said, "When you eat of this tree; you shall die. You will be separated from Me as your true Self." (see Ephesians 2:1; 4:17-18)

Instead of having father God's protection, glory, and love covering, they are naked and ashamed. When we abandoned God through sin, shame came inside of man and they saw that they were uncovered. Before sin came in, there was no shame or sense of nakedness. After sin came in; selfishness became their nature and they sowed the seed of abandonment into the hearts of their descendants. Whatever a man sows, that shall he reap. (see Galatians 6:7)

> *The true self died in the day that Adam and Eve ate from the tree of the knowledge of good and evil.*
> *The false self now became their identity and this false self is based on a lie. This lie says that you can "Be"(exist) apart from the "Being"(life-giver) of God in you*

Abandonment is the fruit of being selfish and independent. The deep sense of responsibility does not affect any independent selfish person. What is this deep sense of responsibility? Well, it is the inner knowing that you have a God given responsibility to love and care for your fellow man, and especially if they are your own children. The true self died in the day that Adam and Eve ate from the tree of the knowledge of good and evil. The false self now became their identity and this false self is based on a lie. This lie says that you can "Be"(exist) apart from the "Being"(life-giver) of God in you. In other words, you do not need God's life in you. Abandonment is an accumulative wound containing the effects of our wounds stemming all the way back from childhood. Abandonment is a feeling of aloneness, of being isolated, and of being deserted within a relationship. The feelings of being abandoned can be so devastating that some youth commit murder or suicide after their mate leaves them. Abandonment overlaps bereavement in that they both involve loss. The one who is abandoned feels the loss just as deep as an individual that is bereaving a loved one.

> *The more we truly love someone, the more that person can hurt or devastate us. The deeper the love, the deeper the possible wound.*

In bereavement, the person who is still living knows that the loved-one has gone to another place appointed unto all men. Although with rejection and abandonment, the person living never seems to get the needed feeling of closure. Being left, ignored, or abandoned has a way of just cutting a person to the very core of their innermost being. We can lose our loved one, but we can also lose our very sense of being, with that loss. Our well-being is now replaced by self-rejection and self-hatred. The more we truly love someone, the more that person can hurt or devastate us. The deeper the love, the deeper the possible wound. The Father has such a deep love for us that He was deeply hurt by mankind loving other gods and ignoring Him as the true God and loving father. Could we really hurt the Father's heart so deeply that he was sorry that he made us? (see Genesis 6:6)

How much pain could a divine heart that is filled with eternal love endure for the sake of His children? We will never really know how much pain God endures for the love of His children.

Let us consider what took place in God's heart after we abandoned him.

1. "Adam where are you?" – a sense of aloneness. He missed his son's presence and dialogue.

2. Father could no longer cover them with his love and so sin now became their covering.

3. Another being took the place of the Father (see John 8:38, 44). That being took the real Father's place.

4. Instead of their body being an expression of the Father's eternal life, they now became an expression for death.

5. The mind of man became more and more corrupt and man threw out the very thoughts of Father God's love and kindness towards them (see Genesis 6:5-7). Their false father now started to fill their minds with the thoughts of hate, violence, and murder for their brothers and sisters and towards God.

6. The Father's heart became deeply pierced because the rejection and rebellion was at the highest level.

7. The pain of rejection only increased as time went on and Father God would share it with his servants, the prophets (see Ezekial 6:9, Hosea 11:1-10, Jer. 2:5-7, Jeremiah 2:11, 2:32)

8. The eternal Son came to earth to take all of his Father's pain and sorrow and shame.

In summary, our Creator had a plan to have a creation in His very own image that would reveal his pure unselfish love to each other. In fulfilling His eternal plan of loving each other, there would be a Utopian world filled with peace, joy, righteousness, love and satisfaction. All creatures would find fulfillment and meaning and purpose while they were united with pure love in the depths of their heart. Father asked one of his children, "where is your brother?" His reply which had already been poisoned by the virus called sin was, "Am I my brother's keeper?" The computer had been infected with a virus called selfishness and now the Master Designer has a cleansing agent called, the blood of the Lamb. All that will come under the fountain will find complete cleansing and now their vessels can once again be

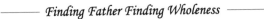

a container for pure love. "In that day there shall be a fountain opened to the house of David and to the inhabitants of Jerusalem for sin and for uncleanness." (Zechariah 13:1).

CHAPTER 11
GOD'S ABANDONED HEART

I am a young Christian woman of the age of 30. No one has ever been so desperate about seeking answers to life's questions than I have been because of my tough childhood. I sought for these answers both in the secular world before I became a Christian and later in the church. Reading the book, The Lamb`s Heart has greatly affected me. I had this overwhelming fear of rejection, anxiety, and the desire to control everyone and everything around me. As I read about the beauty of the broken heart, I literally wept that night on discovering that I do not need to carry this burden on my own or even try to fix myself. I realized that I can trust the heart of the lamb with my pain and inner struggles; I can be vulnerable to him and yet have no fear of being rejected. His gentleness, kindness, and humility are my safety. He does not break a bruised reed in this world. Wow! This was a revelation for me. Even though I had read this before in the Bible I never quite understood it like I did that night. Surely God is more than willing and capable to heal any kind of wounds we have experienced in this life, because none of them are strange to him. That night I chose to stop trying to fix myself (it never works anyway). I felt like a heavy weight had been lifted off my shoulders and lightness replaced it. Where I am now is definitely not where I started. Even though I cannot exactly explain what has happened to me, I know Step by step God is healing my heart.

– Charity, Uganda

From the beginning the Lord desired intimate times with his son, Adam. God the Father wanted an intimate loving relationship with all his sons and daughters. He desired that his children would be over all the works of His hands. He yearned for his sons and daughters to have dominion over everything that walks on earth. It was always in the depth of his eternal heart to share all things with his beloved children. He said it is not good for man to be alone (see Genesis 2:18, 3:8-9). "Adam where are you"? Many children that God has purposed to be in his family have even thrown God out of their thought life.

"Every imagination of the thoughts of his heart was only evil continually", (Genesis 6:5b). Think about that, the entire creation except a few individuals literally threw their Creator out of their thoughts and refused to think about Him. How would this make you feel if the one you passionately loved refuses to ever think about you? Even in the time of their rebellion God was concerned about his children. *"The children of Israel sighed by reason of their bondage and they cried and their cry came up unto God by reason of their bondage. And God heard their groanings and God looked upon the children and God had respect for them."* (Exodus 2:23-25) NIV.

There was only one way to enter into the glorious destiny that is ours. This way is through the Son and his heart of love. Jesus said that no man comes to the Father, but through me. (John 14:6). Children created to rule and reign with their Creator and to reveal his own image to all of creation. A glorious destiny and calling in this world. Father is yearning for an intimate relationship of love and so he made us with a need and capacity to love. God missed the times of walking in the garden with his son, Adam. His heart is filled with love and this unselfish kind of love cannot survive without someone to give it to. This pure love must flow out to others. When selfishness or sin entered into man's heart, then pure love had to go out. It cannot stay in a selfish heart. It must give out love, but selfish hearts must keep in love, instead of giving out love. Now, this glorious eternal plan of the Creator was thwarted by sin and so man's thoughts became filled with hate, instead of love.

The children of God have always been bent on back sliding away from their heavenly Father. One of the tasks of the prophets was to call God's children to come back to their Father God.

> *"Hear oh heavens and give ear oh earth for the Lord has spoken. I have nourished and brought up children, and they have rebelled against me."*
>
> (Isaiah 1:2).

> *"When Israel was a child, I loved him, and out of Egypt I called my son. But the more they were called, the more they went away from me. They sacrificed to the Baals and they burned incense to images. It was I who taught Ephraim to walk, taking them by the arms; but they did not realize it was I who healed them. I led them with cords of human kindness, with ties of love. To them I was like one who lifts a little child to the cheek, and I bent down to feed them. "Will they not return to Egypt and will not Assyria rule over them because they refuse to repent? My people are determined to turn from me. Even though they call me God Most High, I will by no means exalt them. "How can I give you up, Ephraim? How can I hand you over, Israel? How can I treat you like Admah? How can I make you like Zeboyim? My heart is changed within me; all my compassion is aroused."*
>
> (Hosea 11:1-5, 7-8) NIV

Father God has often stooped down to pick up one of his precious children that have fallen. Many times, there is no acknowledging that it was God that protected, restored, and healed them. There is something in the heart of a person that causes them to turn away from Father God, instead of turning toward him. Jeremiah 31:3b says, *"Yea, I have loved thee with an everlasting love, therefore with loving-kindness have I drawn thee"*. The more Father God would call his children to come back to him, the more that they would run away from him. Even the spiritual father Paul had to speak on God's behalf and say to the believers in Corinth, *"...Be reconciled to God"* (2 Corinthians 5:20).

Father God told Jeremiah that his people have forgotten Him days without number. *"Can a maid forget her ornaments or a bride her attire? Yet my people have forgotten me days without number."* (Jeremiah 2:32). Another time God told Jeremiah to ask the people what did he (God), do wrong that would cause them to go so far from Him. *"Thus saith the Lord, What iniquity have your fathers found in me, that they are gone far from me, and have walked after vanity, and are become vain?"* (Jeremiah 2:5) The Lord mentioned to Ezekiel that he was torn to pieces because of the adulterous love affairs that his children had with other gods (see Ezekiel 6:9). Even though the ones that the Father is yearning to love and care for, keep turning away, he still reaches out his arms that are full of compassion.

Many times the very people that God has been trying to heal, love, and restore are instead blaming him for their calamities. Isaiah said that every single person chooses to go his own way and not the way of God. Still, the father puts all of their selfish iniquity on his Son, so that by his stripes (beatings) we could all be healed (Isaiah 53:5-6). God's heart always desired that a family would love, cover, bless, and intimately enjoy each other's presence. This is only possible if the love of God is filling this family. A thought came into Cain's mind that was definitely not from Father. This thought said *"Am I my brother's keeper?"* (see Genesis 4:9b, 1 John 3:12).

I believe that there is one main story that Jesus shared that would reveal the original plan of God for his creation. This is the story of the prodigal son (see Luke 15). Some descriptions from Webster's dictionary to define prodigal is characterized by: profuse or wasteful spending, lavish, yielding abundantly, and luxuriant lifestyle. One synonym listed for prodigal is extravagant. It is possible to even suggest that the father was prodigal. Why? Because he gave so extravagantly to his son. He gave his son an abundance of love and blessings. When his son asked for his inheritance now, while his father was still alive, the father gave it to him. The father had to be a great giver because the son remembered that his father's slaves had plenty of abundance of bread. (see Luke 15:17). He lavished love, gentleness and compassion on his son. God loves a cheerful giver and no one gives more abundantly and cheerfully than God himself. The first response of this father was to pour out mercy, love, kisses and healing on his son as soon as he saw him a long way's off.

Prayer:

Father, right now I ask that you would heal us of memories in our childhood or life of an authority figure that did not enjoy giving to us. Thank you for healing my heart so that I can know you more accurately as a cheerful giver.

It seems that the younger son (prodigal) had a free spirit, one that is filled with excitement, passion and also selfishness. Out of his quest to experience life, he did something that would have been unthinkable at that time within the Jewish culture. To ask his living father for his inheritance would have been a great insult as he did. This request would have been a radical departure from the traditions of his ancestors. It is as if this younger son was saying, "Father, give me now what I will one day receive for my inheritance because I do not want to wait. I want to live and enjoy life now". God, our heavenly father desires that we enjoy all things now (see 1 Timothy 6:17). The problem is that joy can only be experienced in the unselfish love nature of God and not in the selfish nature of man. It is more blessed to give than to receive Jesus said to his followers (see Acts 20:35). True blessing comes when someone pours out love on others. Paul said that we were to do everything in love. "Let all your things be done with charity." (1 Cor. 16:14). Love or charity is an unselfish act with intent to bless and edify others. An unselfish heart will seek to be used as a vessel for God. Selfish people will be tormented if others do not treat them good, but unselfish people will only seek to love others. Haman in the book of Esther was made the highest of all King Ahasuerus's princes (see Esther 3:1). The one thing that Haman lacked, was the joy that is the result of an unselfish heart (see Esther 5:13). His heart was tormented because of his own selfishness.

In the midst of the father's pain over his prodigal son was humiliation and sorrow; he generously sells the inheritance so that he can give his son his portion to take with him to a distant land. It appears that this younger son was probably not intending to return from his new adventurous life that he had chosen.

How about the older son? How did he react to his brother safely returning home? We would have to assume by his reaction to his brother's safe return that he served his father out of a sense of responsibility and legalism instead of joy and love. He probably scolded his younger brother often, over how to do or not to do things, stating that his father would not be happy. He probably pointed out to his brother all of the ways that he was failing his father. I would have to guess that the older brother was not a happy person and there were many times he also wished for a fun-filled life (see Luke 15:28-29). I suppose quite a few times the father would have loved for his sons to know how much he cared for them. I feel certain that the father could sense his younger son's displeasure with the life he was now living at home. His father also would have sensed the older brother's lack of joy and affection. Well, the father had to allow his son to make choices and so he sent him off to his chosen path in life. When the father sees his son returning a long way off, he immediately starts to run to greet him. This meant that every morning the father would have been outside watching to see if today is the day, that my son would come home. Finally the day arrives and his father runs all the way to his son and falls on his neck kissing him. We see in his father's reaction to his son's return, a determined and active love he had to receive, restore, and redeem his son back into the family. There was no mention of past failure, mistakes, sins, disappointments, or anything else that could possibly hinder a thorough healing in his son's heart. Once again, it was the younger son that abandoned the father. The older brother abandoned his younger brother when he returned home. The one person that did not forsake or abandon anyone was the father. If anyone could have held on to a legal right to abandon and discipline someone it should have been the father. Instead of rebuke, discipline, or anger, we instead only see the pure, compassionate love of God in this father revealed.

Have you experienced the disapproval, anger, frustration or abandonment from your earthly father when you failed? Fathers, maybe as you read this book you are seeing areas where you could have done things differently. You can receive total forgiveness from your heavenly Father and know that he wants to lavish upon you love, mercy, compassion, and restoration?

Prayer to pray as a son or daughter:

Father God, right now I forgive everyone that did not give me compassion, love, and a feeling of being accepted and cared for. I am not a failure because I failed. You still have great hope for me and I receive my healing love right now. Thank you Father God for releasing me from an orphan attitude and healing from all the pains of feeling rejected and abandoned. Also forgive me for thinking that you abandoned me. Thank you for suffering with me and not ever abandoning me.

Prayer to pray as a father:

Dear God, I am sorry for not representing you to my children. Please forgive me and cleanse me from all sense of shame. I want to represent the true father to all people, but especially to my children from this moment on. Fill me fresh with your pure love and compassion. Thank you Father God.

THE LONGING HEART OF GOD
REVEALED IN HOSEA

Just like Jesus told the parable of the prodigal son to reveal the heart of the father towards his wayward, lost children. So God also told the prophet Hosea to marry a prostitute called Gomer to reveal his own love for his adulterous children Israel. Hosea was commanded to love a woman that had other lovers. After years of showing his faithful love to his wife Gomer, she abandons Hosea and returns to her other lovers. This is just how God is abandoned by his people again and again and left for other lovers. Suddenly, Gomer discovers that she has lost everything; her attractiveness, her hope, her livelihood and her ability to survive on her own. She now finds herself on a slave block being auctioned off to the highest bidder.

***

A young Polynesian slave girl was placed on the slave blocks of New Orleans during the Civil War. A wealthy plantation owner riding by in his carriage caught her eyes. He immediately sized up the situation, had compassion on her, and began bidding. The bidding began in the hundreds of dollars but soon reached into the thousands. The leaders of the prostitution syndicate were furious but could do little about it.

Finally, the bidding ended and the stranger had purchased the girl. He finished his paperwork and reached the keys to her chains. He approached her and she immediately spat in his face. He wiped the spittle away and continued to unlock her chains. She cursed him violently. The chains dropped away, and to her utter amazement, he said to her very gently, "Woman, you are free". She was astounded, not knowing what to say or do. She had been purchased from the slave market and set free.

The plantation owner who had redeemed her climbed into his carriage and began to drive away. Overwhelmed, the girl chased after him shouting, "Sir, let me serve you. I want to be your slave". The man stopped his carriage and turned to her. "You cannot be my servant." The girl's face dropped, and she turned to walk away. The gentle hand of her new owner turned her around, and he said, "But you can share my home as my adopted daughter".

***

Those who have been redeemed by the blood of Jesus have also been adopted into the family of God. This wealthy plantation owner paid the price for this girl so that she could now be free to love and serve, not because she was forced to, but because she wanted to. God has always desired people that would want to serve him out of love and not from a legalistic attitude of heart. God wanted his people to behold his tremendous love for them through the prophetic act of love by Hosea buying back his adulterous bride Gomer from the slave block (Hosea 3:1-2, 5). We see the heart of Father God wooing and drawing his adulterous people back to him. How many times have we gone astray and turned away from our heavenly Father's love? How many times have we felt like He did not want to have anything to do with us? While the devil was filling our mind about Father God's thoughts toward us. All of our circumstances are arranged to draw us back to love. His purposes are always to bring us back to the image of perfect love, which is his Son (Rom 8:28-29).

Just like the songwriter of "Come thou Fount" wrote, our Heavenly Father knows our heart and how it is prone to wander. "O to grace how great a debtor daily I am constrained to be. Let thy goodness like a fetter bind my wandering heart to thee; prone to wander, Lord, I feel it, prone to leave the God I love."

Why are our hearts prone or liable to leave and desert the God of love? Here are couple of reasons:

- The devil is always accusing God in our mind and telling us how much God hates us and is angry with us.
- An experience with an earthly father that communicated to us that our fathers do not have time or do not care about their children.

Some different types of fathers that communicate to their children that God does not care about them or he does not have time for them are:

1. An absent father

He is not present due to death, divorce, abandonment or work. This father puts a deep fear into his child that God will abandon him sometime. This child is not able to trust God at all times. There is a deep inner anxiety that when God's love and warmth is needed, it will not be available. Also, the children in these homes usually grow up feeling that it is their own fault that their father is not around. They will blame themselves for their father's absence. Gordon Dalby says "that no pain strikes more deeply into a man's heart than being abandoned emotionally or physically by dad. The father calls forth the masculine in the son. Without this essential input from dad the boy cannot later see himself as a man. Quickly, fearfully the gap between the man's inadequacy and who he longs to become fills with shame. The father wound is a wound of absence. Therefore, it is harder to recognize than other wounds." (Darby)

2. A controlling, domineering, and authoritarian father

They demand obedience to all laws and they focus on outward behavior way more than inward attitude. This will instill into the children fear-based relationships with others. As these children grow up and they then learn to evaluate life according to how others react to them. Only if they are accepted, loved, and appreciated will they feel good about themselves. Although, if people do not give them approval they will be hurt and this pattern of fear-based relationships will be reinforced. Fear becomes a governing factor in the lives of these children as they mature.

3. A father that disdains or hates weakness

The majority of these fathers grew up with a father or mother that also disdained mistakes, emotions, and tears. They were also made to feel bad for anything that was not up to their own parent's standards. Children with these kinds of parents will usually be hard or fearful depending on their temperament. If their temperament is strong, they will be hard on themselves and on others. If their temperament is gentle, they will be fearful of not doing things exactly the way that they should. These children tend to see God as angry, uncaring, and lacking compassion. This will cause them to feel as if they always deserve to be punished.

4. A performance oriented father

A perfectionist standard is placed on the child by this kind of father. If this is in a Christian father then he will sincerely feel that we must do our best to be a good Christian. Unfortunately, the standard quickly changes from doing your best in peace and joy, to being the best at what you do. We should do our best and if we score 92 out of 100 answers correct, then we should consider this fantastic. We should not be bound by the idea that we must be the best. The attitude of the heart becomes harder as this person tries to accomplish the highest standard in everything that they do. There are many emotional, physical and mental diseases that will result from growing up in this kind of environment. For example, depression, suicidal thoughts, and burn-out are just a few of the consequences of living in a house with performance oriented parents. Many children will only feel that they deserve love if they accomplish all of their outward goals. These children will struggle internally with deep seated issues of shame and guilt when they do not achieve these goals.

5. A passive father

I have personally witnessed an entire room of people come forward in a meeting to be set free from passivity. Growing up in a house with a passive father is far more common than you might think. Many of these fathers are present physically, but not present emotionally for their families. They also do not make the necessary choices for leading the family and so there is confusion in the atmosphere in this home. Shame and fear are always involved in a passive life. Many children will judge their father for being passive and not taking the lead in the house. Our judgments will block us from entering into all that God has planned for our life (see the author's other books, *Called to be Kings and Priests and The Key to Staying in Love*). A child with a passive father does not feel covered and safe. Children with passive fathers will tend to see God as an uninvolved, uncaring father. If a mother is dominating and controlling and the father is passive, then a child could resent his father for not being his covering from the cruelty of his mother. It is the father's role to cover his children, but a pasiive father does not provide adequate spiritual covering for his family due to his passive nature.

6. An abusive father

These fathers will uncover their precious children through emotional, physical, mental, sexual or spiritual abuse. Many times an abused child will receive spirits from the abuser. The spirit will enter in at the time of abuse in order to use the individual that was abused at a later time. This is why many abused children will in turn abuse others. Spirits are driving them to hurt others until they are healed and forgive the ones that abused them. These people will almost always have a spirit of trauma that will trigger their memories and cause them to feel the pain. Much pain from past trauma is located in the spine and this creates stress in the individual.

Often, these individuals have a soft heart inside, but the evil one tries to destroy the compassion and love from flowing out of their soft heart. These abused children, if they allow father God to heal them, will become tremendous vessels in the hands of God. Their Heavenly father will pour his love and compassion through these people and they will be able to feel the pain of others. Since they themselves have suffered so much pain in their life they have a capacity to receive compassion at a level that is usually much higher than others. The abuse will result in anger and bitterness if it is not healed within a person's life. You have probably heard the statement that "abused people abuse people". In other words, we tend to do to others what has been done to us. If we are blocked from receiving Father God's love and healing, this will definitely result in hurting others as this person grows up in life.

There is a principle behind most anger in the world. The principle is that we will give our anger to those people that we feel have to take it from us. If I think the person I am going to scream at, or hit, or curse will not tolerate my anger, then I will probably keep my anger to myself. Although if I feel this person will tolerate my anger (because

I am much stronger, wiser, wealthier, or carry a badge of authority) then I will "let him have it". We tend to express our anger to those people that have to tolerate it from us. Therefore, if we were abused as a child, there probably was not anyone that this little child could express its deep angry feelings to. As this small child grows up with its buried anger, there will be some individuals that they can express it towards. Some possible candidates that might have to tolerate our buried anger would be: school mates, boyfriend, girlfriend, spouse, children, or etc. All these types of fathers block children from receiving Father God as a loving, caring, and compassionate daddy. When a person is reborn one thing that happens to them is the Son's spirit comes into their inner being crying, "Daddy, Daddy". *"For ye have not received the spirit of bondage again to fear, but ye have received the spirit of adoption whereby we cry, Abba Father."* (Romans 8:15)

"And because you are sons, God has sent forth the Spirit of his Son into your hearts, crying Abba Father." (Galatians 4:6)

God is constantly trying to bring his creation back to his plan for a family in which he is the loving and supreme source. *"And when all things shall be subdued unto him, then shall the Son also himself, be subject unto him that put all things under him, so that God may be all in all."* (1 Corinthians 15:28)

At this very time in history with all the fire of hatred exploding everywhere, there is also another Fire that has been released from heaven. Our God is a consuming fire. (see Hebrews 12:29)

> *"I kept looking until thrones were set up, and Ancient of Days took His seat; His garment was white as snow. And the hair of his head like pure wool. His throne was flames of fire, its wheels were a burning fire. A river of fire was flowing and coming out from before him."*
>
> (Daniel 7:9-10a Amplified Bible)

> *"Its flashes are flashes of fire, a most vehement flame (the very flame of the Lord). Many waters cannot quench love nor can floods drown*

it. If a man would offer all the riches of his house for love, it would
utterly scorned and despised."

(Song of Solomon 8:6c-7 Amplified)

A fire goes before the Lord and burns all of his enemies (see Psalm
97:3)

All the enemies of pure love will be consumed by this all-consuming
fire that burns in the heart of God. The eyes of the Lord are ranging
throughout the whole earth to show himself mighty and strong within
a people whose hearts are set on His fatherly heart (see 2 Chronicles
16:9). The only answer is to destroy the hate that is everywhere is this
pure fire of God's love. Every individual must choose whether he will
accept and embrace the heart of love or reject, despise, and turn away
from it.

May you choose to embrace the fire of love no matter what your
experience has been. It does not matter if you have been the abuser
or the abused. The source of all abuse is in the nature of pride and
selfishness and the source of all healing is humility and pure love.
Humility always precedes honor and pride always precedes destruction
(see Proverbs 18:12).

THE BROKEN WOUNDED HEART OF THE FATHER

All the way to the cross the Son of God carried his Father's broken
heart.

> *"Because for thy sake I have born reproach! Shame has covered my*
> *face. I am become a stranger unto my brethren, and alien to my*
> *mother's children. For the zeal of thine house has eaten me up, and*
> *the reproaches of them that reproached Thee have fallen upon me."*
> (Psalm 69:7-9)

Why was Jesus so filled with zeal that it literally ate him up on
the inside? What is the house that he is referring to? Is it a physical
building that is made by men? Was Jesus consumed by a fiery heart for

a physical building or was it for the true house of God? The true house of God is the place where the Father always desired to live. Please read the following Scriptures: Hebrews 3:6, Acts 7:48-51, Acts 17:24-25, Isaiah 66:1-2, Psalm 90:1, Psalm 132:4-5, 11-14; Acts 3:29-36

The Father always desired to have a special people that he could call his special treasure.

> *"Now therefore if you will obey my voice indeed and keep my covenant, then you shall be a special treasure to me above all people, for all the earth is mine. And you shall be to me kingdom of priests and a holy nation."*
>
> (Exodus 19:5-6a)

In the very beginning the Triune God (Father, Word, and Spirit) said *"let us make man in our image after our likeness, and let them have dominion over everything on earth"* (Genesis 1:26). Before there ever was something called time, the father had a plan for a family in his very own image and likeness.

> *"Bless be the God and father of our Lord Jesus Christ who has blessed us with every spiritual blessing in the heavenly places in Christ, just as he chose us in Him before the foundation of the world, that we should be holy and without blame before him in love having predestined us to adoption as sons by Jesus Christ to himself, according to the good pleasure of his will."*
>
> (Ephesians 1:3-6)

A special people that God could say were His very own treasure and that He was their very own God. This is what the Bible refers to as a special covenant relationship. Many times, the prophets would remind the people that the purpose of their covenant was so God could have a people that he could call his very own and they in turn could call him "their God". The one biblical character that seemed to have the greatest revelation about the essence of a blood covenant, which is to make two parties as they were one, was David. He used the term "my God" more than any other person in the Bible. He also clearly understood that an uncircumcised Philistine like Goliath was an enemy of anyone that was in covenant with the true living God. Therefore he could never overcome anyone that was bound in covenant relationship to God. This is the reason David seemed shocked that God's covenant people, the Israelite army were terrified because of one "tiny" soldier that was uncircumcised. Why did David refer to circumcision, the cutting off of the male foreskin? Circumcision was a sign of being in covenant with almighty God (see 1 Samuel 17).

David had a deep desire in his heart and that was to build a magnificent house for the Lord. However, God had another desire that was in His pure holy heart. Father God wanted to build David a house. He desired to build David's kingdom and exalt his throne forever with one of David's seeds on the throne forever.

> *"And since the time that I commanded judges to be over my people Israel. Moreover I will subdue all thine enemies. Furthermore I tell thee that the Lord will build thee an house. And it shall come to pass, when thy days be expired that thou must go to be with thy fathers, that I will raise up thy seed after thee, which shall be of thy sons; and I will establish his kingdom. He shall build me an house, and I will establish his throne forever. I will be his father, and he shall be my son: and I will not take my mercy away from him, as I took it from him that was before thee: But I will settle him in mine house and in my kingdom forever: and his throne shall be established for evermore."*
>
> (1 Chronicles 17:10-14)

Who is this seed that will be called, The Son of David? Who will sit on the Throne of David forever?

"And, behold, thou shalt conceive in thy womb, and bring forth a son, and shalt call his name Jesus. He shall be great, and shall be called the Son of the Highest: and the Lord God shall give unto him the throne of his father David: And he shall reign over the house of Jacob forever; and of his kingdom there shall be no end."

(Luke 1:31-33)

"Men and brethren, let me freely speak unto you of the patriarch David, that he is both dead and buried, and his sepulchre is with us unto this day. Therefore being a prophet, and knowing that God had sworn with an oath to him, that of the fruit of his loins, according to the flesh, he would raise up Christ to sit on his throne; He seeing this before spake of the resurrection of Christ, that his soul was not left in hell, neither his flesh did see corruption. This Jesus hath God raised up, whereof we all are witnesses. Therefore being by the right hand of God exalted, and having received of the Father the promise of the Holy Ghost, he hath shed forth this, which ye now see and hear. For David is not ascended into the heavens: but he saith himself, The Lord said unto my Lord, Sit thou on my right hand, Until I make thy foes thy footstool. Therefore let all the house of Israel know assuredly, that God hath made the same Jesus, whom ye have crucified, both Lord and Christ."

(Acts 2:29-36)

This house that God is building is a temple built by the Holy Spirit in which the very essence and nature of the Son is all and in all.

"For through him we both have access by one Spirit unto the Father. Now therefore ye are no more strangers and foreigners, but fellow citizens with the saints, and of the household of God; And are built upon the foundation of the apostles and prophets, Jesus Christ himself being the chief corner stone; In whom all the building fitly framed together groweth unto an holy temple in the

Lord: In whom ye also are builded together for an habitation of God through the Spirit."

(Ephesians 2:18-22)

Paul prayed in Ephesians 3:14-18 to the Father of our Lord Jesus Christ, of whom all fatherhood is named (actual meaning), that he the father would grant the whole body according to the riches of his glory to be empowered by his Spirit on the inside so that Christ the Son, might dwell in us. To learn the meaning of son-ship is a major calling of the believer on earth. The eternal plan of God was to have sons who would reveal the glory of his unparalleled Son.

"For I reckon that the sufferings of this present time are not worthy to be compared with the glory which shall be revealed in us. For the earnest expectation of the creature waiteth for the manifestation of the sons of God."

(Romans 18-19)

There is a glory that is to be revealed in us, and creation will see the Father when they behold his very glory in his children. A heart that is increasing in pure love is the heart Paul defines as being established in holiness in the Father's presence when he comes in the full glory of his Son (see 1 Thessalonians 3:11-13).

Now, let us return back to the original question. Why was, Jesus filled with such a zeal for his Father's house that it consumed him (see Psalm 69:9)? The house of God had become full of all uncleanness, greed, and evil on the inside; but looking beautiful on the outside (Matthew 23:25-28). Jesus also said that *"his house shall be called a house of prayer, but ye have made it a den of thieves"* (Matthew 21:13b). The house of God lost its purpose to pray and intercede with the heart of a priest. Jesus told his disciples that they have the authority to remit and retain sins in his name. To remit is a priestly function acting on behalf of men. To retain is a kingly function, acting on behalf of the government of heaven (John 20:23). Moses said, *"Pardon I pray thee"* and the Lord responded to him by saying, *"according to your word, I have pardoned"* (Numbers 14:19-20).

> *The Priesthood of the Lamb must start to remit and retain the sins so that in the name of Jesus Christ, the land can be free from the demonic covenants that have been made through sin!*

This priestly, heavenly order of Melchizedek is now starting to manifest the image and authority of the heavenly kingdom (1 Corinthians 15:47-49). As a part of the heavenly order of Melchizedek, we have the privilege and honor of remitting (to bid go away, to depart, to send forth, to send away) or retaining (to have power, to be chief or master, to rule, to take hold of or to seize) sins. Innocent blood is crying out against all people that hate, murder, rape, abuse, abandon, etc. Their innocent blood is crying out for the justice of the law. It is the sin that defiles the land and the land must be cleansed. When the pure, innocent blood of Jesus was spilled on the earth, now his innocent blood is crying out for justice, but this time it is the justice of The Lamb and not the justice of the law. The Priesthood of the Lamb must start to remit and retain the sins so that in the name of Jesus Christ, the land can be free from the demonic covenants that have been made through sin! Sin, torment, sicknesses, disease, addiction, depression and many more such bondages can be broken because of the tremendous power of the pure blood of Jesus. Everyone that believes in Him can be freed and justified from everything that had them bound. (see Romans 3:23-28). Blood has a voice and the blood of Jesus is crying out for mercy! Abel`s innocent blood cries out for vengeance, but Jesus pure blood cries out for mercy

> *This chosen generation will proclaim and reveal another Kingdom that has all power, all authority, pure love, and the mercy of the Father.*

Father God is wanting a chosen generation, a royal priesthood that will declare his righteousness, his triumph, and reveal His glory that was fulfilled at the cross (see 1 Peter 2:9, John 20:23, Romans 3:25). This Heavenly priesthood is now coming forth with the power of Jesus, like Stephen, who full of faith and power did great wonders and miracles among the people (see Acts 6:8). This chosen generation will proclaim and reveal another Kingdom that has all power, all authority, pure love, and the mercy of the Father. Stephen with almost no breath remaining in him, cried with a loud voice, *"Lord lay not this sin to their charge. And when he had said this, he fell asleep"* (Acts 7:60). After Stephen cried out with a loud voice for God to remit their sins, he then died.

This immediately reminds us of another one that also cried out, *"Father forgive them, for they know not what they do"* (Luke 23:34). The tense that is used for this word, *"forgive them"*, is in the imperative. This means that Jesus is actually speaking as a command to his Father. As if he was saying, "Father you must forgive them". I am deeply convicted when I think of Paul begging for the salvation of those Jews that hated him (see Romans 9:1-3). Moses also said, "if you can't forgive; then blot me out of your book" (see Exodus 32:32). Jesus commanded forgiveness for those people that hated him. Stephen commanded forgiveness to those people that were stoning him. Moses pleaded for God to have mercy on his people, then said, if you cannot save them, I do not want to go to heaven either. Paul begged for mercy for the very people that would have loved to see him dead. What love, what incredible love is in these men of God? It is the very same pure, holy love of the Father who never delights in the death of the wicked. *"Have I any pleasure at all that the wicked should die? saith the Lord God: and not that he should return from his ways, and live?"* (Ezekiel 18:23). God's heart is full of compassion. *"The Lord is gracious and full of compassion"* (Psalm 145:8a).

To be full means, that there is no room for any other substance. The word compassion means to suffer with. This is saying that the Lord always suffers with every person in their pain and he feels what they are feeling. The first question that would arise is; why doesn't God stop all the suffering? I find it quite amazing that when the subject of pain and suffering is discussed, so often the person that receives the majority of blame is Father God. Why not ask why did mankind choose to be selfish? What is the devil's part in suffering? Why do so few individuals never consider God's pain and agony? How did the Father feel when he was beholding his greatest treasure, his most beloved, pure Son being massacred, ripped open, spit upon, and beaten with the most severe hatred ever? How did Father God feel when he had to utterly forsake for the first time ever his dear Son (see Psalm 22:1)? This took place shortly after Jesus told his disciples, you will all abandon me. *"Behold, the hour comes, is now come, that ye shall be scattered, every man to his own and shall leave me alone; and yet I am not alone because the Father is with me"* (John 16:32, Matt. 27:46).

So, why does God allow so much suffering in this world? The Creator's plan was to have sons and not slaves. A son must freely choose to honor, love and obey the one that he loves. A slave can be forced to obey the rules and God could have easily forced His creation to obey. Father God did not want to control and force his children to obey Him, therefore he had a plan that would involve a family that delighted to do his will. When it is clearly understood that the will of God is eternally satisfying and joyful, it is no longer be a burden to do his will. As soon as a person chooses its own will over the will of its Father, self-will becomes the master. Self-will is another description of sin and when someone chooses his selfish will; he loses touch with the realm of the kingdom of God. If the creation (angels and men) were allowed to simply do what they think is best, this could only result in selfish rebellion and anarchy. In a kingdom, the king must have the power and wisdom to rule his domain. It is only through the nature of the Son that we can delight in God's will. Our own selfish nature does not delight in the will of God (see Romans 8:7-8; Hebrews 10:6-8, 13:20-21, Phillipians 2:13). Jesus said, *"he who has the Son has the life"* (1 John 5:11). Do I want to be a son or a slave? One day every knee will be forced to bow to the king.

Why so much suffering? Sin came into the world and by its very nature, pain and death became a part of man's very existence. Take away self-will and replace it with pure love; would there have been suffering in the world? No, self-will or sin is the cause of suffering in the world. The heart of the Father is the glory that God revealed to Moses (Exodus 33:18-21, 34:5-8). This is the heart of the eternal Lamb that was slain before man was created. Beholding the deep love and compassion that was displayed by Jesus, Moses, Paul, Stephen, and others, we are starting to understand what the father's heart is really like. Sons must choose his heart so that they can be merciful as their Father in heaven is merciful.

> *"But love ye your enemies, and do good, and lend, hoping for nothing again; and your reward shall be great, and ye shall be the children of the Highest: for he is kind unto the unthankful and to the evil. Be ye therefore merciful, as your Father also is merciful."*
>
> (Luke 6:35-36)

We do not have this kind of love inside of us, but we can choose it and trust the Holy Spirit to express it through our body. I believe it was this extreme humility and love in the heart of Jesus Christ that stirred up the Pharisees to respond in hate. This extreme lowly heart of the Lamb (Matthew 11:29) causes a chain reaction in the spiritual world. Pride is the nature of selfish men and God's presence must resist all selfish pride. This is why satan knows that men are helpless as long as they choose to walk in pride. Therefore, pride is the greatest tool that Satan has to defeat the church (see Job 41:34, Job 40:9-14, Matt. 23:12, Prov. 16:5, Prov. 16:18, Acts 12:23). (Note: For more understanding on pride, see author's other books.) When someone humbles themself, the spirits working through the pride of another person are bound. This is why Jesus could walk through a murderous, raging, and angry crowd that wanted to kill him without injuries (see Luke 4:28-30). Humility always overcomes pride and has the protective power of Heaven surrounding it. (see Psalms 34:7, Isaiah 66:2b)

When we humble ourselves, God exalts us (see Matthew 23:12) Peter said that the Body should clothe itself with humility and then God will exalt them at the right time (see 1Peter 5:5-6). God himself so loves humility that He will draw near to the humble and allow their heart to be His dwelling place (see Isaiah 57:15, Psalm 34:18, James 4:6-8). When Christ's humility is operating in us, which is dead to self, this death is also working to impart life into others (see 2 Corinthians 4:12). From the beginning of time, Father has had an ancient way that he always desired his children to walk on and this is called, the ancient path. This is the way into the Father's pure, holy heart and this way is the heart of the Lamb of God, who is in the bosom of the Father. (see John 1:18). The lowly heart of the Lamb is exalted for all eternity and one day, all of creation will clearly behold His magnificent glory. (This will be discussed more in the section on the ancient path into the Father's heart.)

Publication bibliography
Darby, Gordon: Father Wounds. Available online at http://rustyrustenbach.blogspot.de/2013/06/father-hunger-on-fathers-day-2013.html.

CHAPTER 12
THE CATACLYSMIC COLLISION OF TWO WORLDS

I always found when I had to be around people, I had to work myself up just to be with them. I hated it, the feeling of these needy people; vulnerable people with an open heart that Jesus delighted in. I struggled with just being around them. I would ask the Lord "Why Lord? Why does this bother me so much?" He has shown me that although I would go to Jesus with my prayers, seek the Holy Spirit, He would minister to me in my woundedness and reveal to me my hidden and hard places of pride. But hardness would come out of me to the people that God would want me to minister to. As I continued to seek God on what was going on, He showed me that what I lacked was the intimacy and compassion that only comes from knowing the Father. After many, many stirrings to consider the truth of this; the Father had to take me back to the place with my own father. I could not remember many times as a young girl that I had interaction with my father. There was just no connection. Just a man in the house; but no special words, pet names, a lap to crawl on, no one to speak "you are special or a precious gem." Ironically, there was also no harshness from him either, no mean words, no heavy discipline; in fact there was no discipline, no interaction, no intimacy, and no compassion. My Heavenly Father is so wonderful. He had to remind me of all of this so then He could start the work in me. I choose to come to the truth that He has and still is showing me that the lack of intimacy and compassion with my own father was the reason that I could not connect with the Father. I tried and tried to connect to the Father but could not. I hated this hardness in me and realizing that there was not anything I could do, but it was what He was going to do in me. Was I willing? After a fearful yes, "I am willing", the Father came in slowly and bit by bit to show me a love He had for me, an intimacy and compassion He shows for me. Only He can work these changes in me, but I had to come to truth and deal with any hidden lies. Is this easy, no. Is it worth it; yes. As my intimacy and compassion grow with my Father, my intimacy and compassion keep growing for the people that God truly loves. I am so thankful for all that He has been doing in my life.

— Susan B, Wisconsin, USA

Two worlds are now colliding! At the present time, there is a cataclysmic collision taking place in the invisible world and it is the colliding of two opposing kingdoms. The word cataclysmic means large-scale and violent and the word collide means to come into conflict or opposition. Some synonyms of collide are: conflict, be in conflict, be in opposition, differ, diverge, disagree, be at variance, be at odds, and be incompatible. The Scriptures describe a kingdom called, "this world" and it is the domain of satan. There is also another realm where the Father rules. In this realm His ways are exalted and this realm is called the Kingdom of God. These two worlds, realms, or kingdoms are in direct opposition to each other. Jesus said, *"My kingdom is not of this world: if my kingdom were of this world, then would my servants fight, that I should not be delivered to the Jews: but now is my kingdom not from hence."* (John 18:36)

Jesus Christ came as the true King of the Jews. *"Now when Jesus was born in Bethlehem of Judaea in the days of Herod the king, behold, there came wise men from the east to Jerusalem, saying, Where is he that is born King of the Jews? For we have seen his star in the east, and are come to worship him. When Herod the king had heard these things, he was troubled, and all Jerusalem with him"* (Matthew 2:1-3). It is thought by many people that these three wise men from the east were kings. Whatever they were, it is certain that they were very prestigious and wealthy. The gifts that they brought such as gold and frankincense were gifts that one would bestow on a king. These men knew that this one was "born" king. At his very birth, he was the true king!

> *At this present moment, the true King is exalted at the Father's right hand of power.*

At this present moment, the true King is exalted at the Father's right hand of power. In Matthew 28:18-20, Jesus spoke to His disciples saying, *"All power is given unto me in heaven and in earth. Go ye therefore, and teach all nations, baptizing them in the name of the Father, and of the Son, and of the Holy Ghost: Teaching them to observe all things whatsoever I have commanded you: and, lo, I am with you always, even unto the end of the world. Amen."*

Oswald Chambers said, "Never seek after anything other than the approval of God, and always be willing to go *"outside the camp, bearing His reproach"* (see Hebrews 13:13). In Luke 10:20, Jesus told the disciples not to rejoice in successful service, and yet this seems to be the one thing in which most of us do rejoice in. We have a commercialized view – we count how many souls have been saved and sanctified, we thank God, and then we think everything is all right. Yet our work only begins where God's grace has laid the foundation. Our work is not to save souls, but to disciple them. Salvation and sanctification are the work of God's sovereign grace, and our work as His disciples is to disciple others' lives until they are totally yielded to God. One life totally devoted to God is of more value to Him than one hundred lives which have been simply awakened by His Spirit. As workers for God, we must reproduce our own kind spiritually, and those lives will be God's testimony to us as His workers. God brings us up to a standard of life through His grace, and we are responsible for reproducing that same standard in others." (Chambers 1992)

Jesus commanded us to go and proclaim his kingdom wherever we go. The difficulty with that is there is another kingdom that has been ruling over this world system for a long time and it is the mandate for every Christian to declare another ruling kingdom on earth.

"This Jesus hath God raised up, whereof we all are witnesses. Therefore being by the right hand of God exalted, and having received of the Father the promise of the Holy Ghost, he hath shed forth this, which ye now see and hear. For David is not ascended into the heavens: but he saith himself, The Lord said unto my Lord, Sit thou on my right hand."

(Acts 2:32-34)

"Him hath God exalted with his right hand to be a Prince and a Saviour, for to give repentance to Israel, and forgiveness of sins."

(Acts 5:31)

"And being found in fashion as a man, he humbled himself, and became obedient unto death, even the death of the cross. Wherefore God also hath highly exalted him, and given him a name which is above every name: That at the name of Jesus every knee should bow, of things in heaven, and things in earth, and things under the earth;"

(Phil. 2:8-10)

Satan is known as the "god" of this present world, but his kingdom is only as powerful as his demonic reign over the lives of individuals. Jesus Christ clearly and forcefully declared that the prince of this world comes for him, but he had nothing in him! *"Hereafter I will not talk much with you: for the prince of this world cometh, and hath nothing in me"* (John 14:30). The Christian is also commanded to give no place to the devil (see Ephesians 4:27). Presently, everything in heaven and earth is being shaken; but why are the heavens also experiencing a shaking? The reason is because everything that is manifesting on earth first has its origin in the heavens.

"And I also say to thee, that thou art a rock, and upon this rock I will build my assembly, and the gates of Hades shall not prevail against it; and I will give to thee the keys of the reign of the heavens, and whatever thou mayest bind upon the earth shall be having been

bound in the heavens, and whatever thou mayest loose upon the earth shall be having been loosed in the heavens."

(Matthew 16:18-19 YLT)

"And the seventy returned again with joy, saying, Lord, even the devils are subject unto us through thy name. And he said unto them, I beheld Satan as lightning fall from heaven. Behold, I give unto you power to tread on serpents and scorpions, and over all the power of the enemy: and nothing shall by any means hurt you. Notwithstanding in this rejoice not, that the spirits are subject unto you; but rather rejoice, because your names are written in heaven. In that hour Jesus rejoiced in spirit, and said, I thank thee, O Father, Lord of heaven and earth, that thou hast hid these things from the wise and prudent, and hast revealed them unto babes: even so, Father; for so it seemed good in thy sight."

(Luke 10:17-21).

"For thus saith the Lord of hosts; Yet once, it is a little while, and I will shake the heavens, and the earth, and the sea, and the dry land; And I will shake all nations, and the desire of all nations shall come: and I will fill this house with glory, saith the Lord of hosts."

(Haggai 2:6-7)

"See that ye refuse not him that speaketh. For if they escaped not who refused him that spake on earth, much more shall not we escape, if we turn away from him that speaketh from heaven: Whose voice then shook the earth: but now he hath promised, saying, Yet once more I shake not the earth only, but also heaven. And this word, Yet once more, signifieth the removing of those things that are shaken, as of things that are made, that those things which cannot be shaken may remain. Wherefore we receiving a kingdom which cannot be moved, let us have grace, whereby we may serve God acceptably with reverence and godly fear: For our God is a consuming fire."

(Hebrews 12:25-29)

The Apostle Paul had a clear perception concerning the nature of the invisible world and its eternal conflict between two opposing kingdoms. Receive his revelation as you read the following Scriptures:

> *"Finally, my brethren, be strong in the Lord, and in the power of his might. Put on the whole armour of God, that ye may be able to stand against the wiles of the devil. For we wrestle not against flesh and blood, but against principalities, against powers, against the rulers of the darkness of this world, against spiritual wickedness in high places. Wherefore take unto you the whole armour of God, that ye may be able to withstand in the evil day, and having done all, to stand. Stand therefore, having your loins girt about with truth, and having on the breastplate of righteousness; And your feet shod with the preparation of the gospel of peace; Above all, taking the shield of faith, wherewith ye shall be able to quench all the fiery darts of the wicked. And take the helmet of salvation, and the sword of the Spirit, which is the word of God: Praying always with all prayer and supplication in the Spirit, and watching thereunto with all perseverance and supplication for all saints; And for me, that utterance may be given unto me, that I may open my mouth boldly, to make known the mystery of the gospel, For which I am an ambassador in bonds: that therein I may speak boldly, as I ought to speak."*
> (Ephesians 6:10-20)

The Christian, that is born anew by the Spirit of God; is also walking on earth in his physical body, but at the same time seated with Christ in the heavens.

While Jesus was physically walking on the earth, he was at the same moment, spiritually united with his Father in the heavens. *"And no man hath ascended up to heaven, but he that came down from heaven, even the Son of man which is in heaven."* (John 3:13) The Christian, that is born anew by the Spirit of God; is also walking on earth in his physical body, but at the same time seated with Christ in the heavens.

"Even when we were dead in sins, hath quickened us together with Christ, (by grace ye are saved;) And hath raised us up together, and made us sit together in heavenly places in Christ Jesus: That in the ages to come he might shew the exceeding riches of his grace in his kindness toward us through Christ Jesus."

(Ephesians 2:5-7)

"Buried with him in baptism, wherein also ye are risen with him through the faith of the operation of God, who hath raised him from the dead. And you, being dead in your sins and the uncircumcision of your flesh, hath he quickened together with him, having forgiven you all trespasses; Blotting out the handwriting of ordinances that was against us, which was contrary to us, and took it out of the way, nailing it to his cross; And having spoiled principalities and powers, he made a shew of them openly, triumphing over them in it."

(Colossians 2:12-15)

The spiritual rulers of this world have already been sentenced by the Emperor. This sentence has already occurred. Please consider the following truths from the Holy Scriptures:

"Now is the judgment of this world: now shall the prince of this world be cast out. And I, if I be lifted up from the earth, will draw all men unto me."

(John 12:31-32)

"And when he is come, he will reprove the world of sin, and of righteousness, and of judgment: Of sin, because they believe not on me; Of righteousness, because I go to my Father, and ye see me no more; Of judgment, because the prince of this world is judged."

(John 16:8-11)

See Psalms 2, Revelation 11:15, Isaiah 27:1, Matthew 6:9-13, 3:2, 4:17, 23, 10:7, 12:28, 13:19, Luke 4:33, 6:20, 9:1-2, 9:27, 60, 10:9-

11, 17:20-21, John 3:3, Acts 8:12, 20:25, 28:31, 1 Corinthians 4:20, 15:24, Romans 14:17, Col 1:13.

KINGDOM OF HEAVEN AND VIOLENCE

"And from the days of John the Baptist until now the kingdom of heaven suffereth violence, and the violent take it by force."
(Matthew 11:12)

"The law and the prophets were until John: since that time the kingdom of God is preached, and every man presseth into it."
(Luke 16:16)

"Strive to enter in at the strait gate: for many, I say unto you, will seek to enter in, and shall not be able."
(Luke 13:24)

The word "suffers violence" means: – to use force, to apply force – to force, inflict violence on

These words are implying that to have a share in the heavenly kingdom it must be sought for with the most ardent zeal, and the most intense exertion.

Here are some more words from these Scriptures:
The word Violent means: – Strong, forceful – Using force, violent
The phrase Take it means: – To seize, carry off by force, to seize on, claim for one's self eagerly

Why is it so hard to enter the kingdom?

"Therefore all things whatsoever ye would that men should do to you, do ye even so to them: for this is the law and the prophets. Enter ye in at the strait gate: for wide is the gate, and broad is the way, that

leadeth to destruction, and many there be which go in thereat: Because strait is the gate, and narrow is the way, which leadeth unto life, and few there be that find it. Beware of false prophets, which come to you in sheep's clothing, but inwardly they are ravening wolves. Ye shall know them by their fruits. Do men gather grapes of thorns, or figs of thistles? Even so every good tree bringeth forth good fruit; but a corrupt tree bringeth forth evil fruit. A good tree cannot bring forth evil fruit, neither can a corrupt tree bring forth good fruit. Every tree that bringeth not forth good fruit is hewn down, and cast into the fire. Wherefore by their fruits ye shall know them. Not everyone that saith unto me, Lord, Lord, shall enter into the kingdom of heaven; but he that doeth the will of my Father which is in heaven. Many will say to me in that day, Lord, Lord, have we not prophesied in thy name? and in thy name have cast out devils? and in thy name done many wonderful works? And then will I profess unto them, I never knew you: depart from me, ye that work iniquity."

(Matthew 7:12-23).

"If ye were of the world, the world would love his own: but because ye are not of the world, but I have chosen you out of the world, therefore the world hateth you." (John 15:19). Here Jesus is referring to the world as a spiritual entity, a system with a personality in it. This is why he calls it "his own". The world will love his own. In order to overcome this world, we must understand that within the context of "this world" is a mind with a personality. This personality is a demonic spirit that is self-centered and proud. "Wherein in time past ye walked according to the course of this world, according to the prince of the power of the air, the spirit that now worketh in the children of disobedience"

(Ephesians. 2:2)

In summary, there are two kingdoms and both are colliding at this present moment. Both stand for opposing views, opposing desires, both are serving different rulers and both are rejoicing in everything that the other kingdom grieves over. Truly, these two kingdoms are worlds apart in standard, motives and destiny. Jesus refers to two fathers: satan, the devil and God, the heavenly Father. (John 8:38-44, Matthew 23:9). Each individual must decide which side will they stand on and which father will influence them. If I am a father, then do I want my family to behold God, the father inside of me? If I am a woman, will I let the words, deeds and thoughts of father satan affect me and determine what my life will consist of or will I allow father God to speak his words and reveal his heart towards me? These two worlds are so totally different. Now, is the time for every Christian to stand with the rightful King and Ruler of the universe and to submit to His standards and to reveal his character.

CHAPTER 13

THE REPROACH OF CHRIST

It was the first prayer I ever received: Greg prayed for me and the words got literally branded into my heart – they were full of life and full of God. These words kept pursuing me. The words were as follows: "Lord, give her a heart of compassion and mercy und put her heart really close to your heart." My heart at the time was hard, self-righteous, religious, and I could not feel anything – let alone compassion! Then I read the book "The Lamb's Heart" and cried through every page. I could only take it a page at a time. In this book I saw the lowliness and the mercy of the Lamb. This was the total opposite of my own heart! With my whole being I longed for His heart! Today I am completely changed. "

– Lilli L, North Germany

We read in Exodus 25:8 that God instructed Moses to build a sanctuary for him and he would dwell in their midst. In Exodus 33:7 it says that Moses took the tabernacle and pitched it outside the camp, a long way off and everyone that really wanted to seek the Lord had to go outside the camp to find Him. It is a reproach for God to not be in the midst of his people. Paul describes the importance of God's sons and daughters coming out from the unclean and defiling idolatry that is in the world (see 2 Corinthians 6:15-7:1).

To love the heart of the Lamb is to hate the heart of pride.

When describing the reproach of Christ, the writer of Hebrews associates suffering afflictions as a part of esteeming the reproach of Christ. Moses's choice to suffer affliction with the people of God was a choice to carry and esteem the reproach of Christ. Whenever we identify ourselves with the lowly, meek nature of the Lamb, we are choosing to carry the reproach of God. The entire world system that is under the false god of this world, satan, loves its selfishness and pride. To love the heart of the Lamb is to hate the heart of pride. When a person chooses to love the heart of God they will be mocked by the world. In a few words how can we describe the reproach of Jesus Christ? It is the eternal shame that covers the face of God the Father. The shame that God carries is a result of the hatred coming out of the proud heart of mankind towards the lowly heart of the Lamb of God. Wherever there are Christians that are selfish, they will oppose other Christians that love the heart of the Lamb. This is what Paul is describing about the troubles in the last days that will come upon the world.

> *"But realize this, that in the last days difficult times will come. For men will be lovers of self, lovers of money, boastful, arrogant, revilers, disobedient to parents, ungrateful, unholy, unloving, irreconcilable, malicious gossips, without self-control, brutal, haters of good, treacherous, reckless, conceited, lovers of pleasure rather than lovers of God, holding to a form of godliness, although they have denied its power; Avoid such men as these"*
>
> (2 Timothy 3:1-5).

We read that these people that are lovers of self, boastful, arrogant, unholy, malicious gossips, and etc. are only "holding to a form of godliness" (as seen in previous scripture). This means that they will probably be in a Church building on Sunday.

> *"He is despised and rejected of men; a man of sorrows, and acquainted with grief."*
>
> (Isaiah 53:3a)

"Come to Him [the risen Lord] as to a living Stone which men rejected and threw away, but which is choice and precious in the sight of God."

(1 Peter 2:4 [AMP])

"So, let us go out to Him outside the camp, bearing His contempt [the disgrace and shame that He had to suffer]."

Hebrews 13:13 (AMP)

"Because for Your sake I have borne reproach; Confusion and dishonor have covered my face. I have become estranged from my brothers and an alien to my mother's sons. For zeal for Your house has consumed me, And the [mocking] insults of those who insult You have fallen on me." "You know my reproach and my shame and my dishonor [how I am insulted]; my adversaries are all before You [each one fully known]. Reproach and insults have broken my heart and I am so sick. I looked for sympathy, but there was none, And for comforters, but I found none."

Psalm 69:7-9, 19-20 (AMP).

"And to him they agreed: and when they had called the apostles, and beaten them, they commanded that they should not speak in the name of Jesus, and let them go. And they departed from the presence of the council, rejoicing that they were counted worthy to suffer shame for his name."

(Acts 5: 40-41)

Those things were ·important [valuable; or assets] to me, but now I think they are ·worth nothing [or liabilities; a loss] because of Christ. Not only those things, but I think that all things are ·worth nothing [or liabilities; a loss] ·compared with [or because of] the ·greatness [superior/supreme value] of knowing Christ Jesus my Lord. Because of him, I have lost all those things, and now I ·know they are [consider them] ·worthless trash [garbage; refuse; excrement]. This allows me to have [...so that I may gain] Christ and to ·belong to [be united with; be found in] him."

Philippians 3:7-9 (New Emphasized) "

"Choosing rather to suffer affliction with the people of God, than to enjoy the pleasures of sin for a season; Esteeming the reproach of Christ greater riches than the treasures in Egypt: for he had respect unto the recompence of the reward."

Hebrews 11:25-26

"Now Moses used to take the tent and to pitch it without the camp, afar off from the camp; and he called it, The tent of meeting. And it came to pass, that every one that sought Jehovah went out unto the tent of meeting, which was without the camp." Everything considered unclean was to go outside the camp, lest it defile the camp. The camp is to be holy.

Exodus 33:7

"All the days wherein the plague shall be in him he shall be defiled; he is unclean: he shall dwell alone; without the camp shall his habitation be."

Leviticus 13:46

"And he that is to be cleansed shall wash his clothes, and shave off all his hair, and wash himself in water, that he may be clean: and after that he shall come into the camp, and shall tarry abroad out of his tent seven days."

Leviticus 14:8

"And he that let go the goat for the scapegoat shall wash his clothes, and bathe his flesh in water, and afterward come into the camp. And the bullock for the sin offering, and the goat for the sin offering, whose blood was brought in to make atonement in the holy place, shall one carry forth without the camp; and they shall burn in the fire their skins, and their flesh, and their dung."

Leviticus 16:26-27,

"And the Lord said unto Moses, If her father had but spit in her face, should she not be ashamed seven days? let her be shut out from the camp seven days, and after that let her be received in again. And Miriam was shut out from the camp seven days: and the people journeyed not till Miriam was brought in again."

Numbers 12:14-15

The camp is to be holy because the Lord dwells in the midst of it.

"For the Lord thy God walketh in the midst of thy camp, to deliver thee, and to give up thine enemies before thee; therefore shall thy camp be holy: that he see no unclean thing in thee, and turn away from thee."

Deuteronomy 23:14

Who was the first one to go outside the camp? It was the Holy God himself (see Exodus 33:7). This is the reproach. The people sinned a great sin of idolatry, sexual immorality, and uncleanness; then the Lord went outside the camp.

Jesus Christ carried his father's reproach, which broke his heart open. Although Jesus was perfect, holy, and totally pure in every way; he was treated as an evil, vile blasphemer, idolater, and even called by the religious leaders "the prince of all the demons himself"! He was made Sin, he became a curse and he breathed his last breath as a rejected, condemned criminal that was apparently worthy of such agonizing punishment. All the while, Jesus was carrying the reproach, he knew that it was actually the heart attitudes of the people, especially the people of God which had evil attitudes towards his loving and pure Father. Jesus suffered all that shame for his father's sake and the early church saw the great honor in suffering shame for their Lord's sake. Why has there always been so much shame in carrying the cross?

Hebrews 12:2 says, "Looking unto Jesus the author and finisher of our faith; who for the joy that was set before him endured the cross, despising the shame, and is set down at the right hand of the throne of God."

Since, the kingdoms of this wicked world are in direct opposition to the kingdom of our Christ. This world scorns someone that suffers for others, washes feet, serves, humbles, and makes himself of no reputation in the eyes of others. They only have one word for such a lowly person and that is, "come down from that lowly position of sacrifice and let others serve you" (see Matthew 27:40, 42).

> *"And saying, Thou that destroyest the temple, and buildest it in three days, save thyself. If thou be the Son of God, come down from the cross. He saved others; himself he cannot save. If he be the King of Israel, let him now come down from the cross, and we will believe him."*
>
> (Mark 15:30)

> *Never has this world had such a king and therefore, Jesus's entrance into the world was to bring an entirely different type of kingdom.*

"Save thyself, and come down from the cross." The world says we will not serve a lamb, never will He be our King. We cannot believe that a King can be so humble, lowly, and kind. Kings are supposed to rule people, causing them to honor and serve them and let others know how great they really are. Whoever heard of a king being treated as a slave. Never has this world had such a king and therefore, Jesus's entrance into the world was to bring an entirely different type of kingdom. Many years ago, Father God told his people and all of creation to rejoice greatly because of his true King which was coming with salvation, justice, and deep humility (see Zechariah 9:9). The true anointed King of the universe is still rejected, despised, hated, and misunderstood by the multitudes (see Psalm 2, Isaiah 53:3, Psalm 110 and Daniel 4:17).

His spiritual Body has the honor and privilege to carry his reproach and shame in this world. The Bride desires to be one with her Groom and therefore she wants to feel his heart and bear his pain of rejection and hate. The Lamb's wife is now making herself ready to be completely in perfect union with her beloved.

"Beloved, take not [as] strange the fire [of persecution] which has taken place amongst you for [your] trial, as if a strange thing was happening to you; but as ye have share in the sufferings of Christ, rejoice, that in the revelation of his glory also ye may rejoice with exultation. If ye are reproached in [the] name of Christ, blessed [are ye]; for the [Spirit] of glory and the Spirit of God rests upon you: [on their part he is blasphemed, but on your part he is glorified.] Let none of you suffer indeed as murderer, or thief, or evildoer, or as overseer of other people's matters; but if as a christian, let him not be ashamed, but glorify God in this name."

1 Peter 4:12-16 (Darby)

James 1:12 says, *"Blessed [is the] man who endures temptation; for, having been proved, he shall receive the crown of life, which He has promised to them that love him."* Just like a Queen wears her crown to show her place in the kingdom and heart of her King, so there is a special crown that will be given to those beloved ones that truly suffer and love their King. Isaac Watts knew a beautiful truth about surveying the cross and he wrote about it in his song, 'When I survey'.

"When I survey the wondrous cross on which the Prince of glory died, My richest gain I count but loss, And pour contempt on all my pride. Forbid it, Lord, that I should boast, Save in the death of Christ my God! All the vain things that charm me most, I sacrifice them to His blood. See from His head, His hands, His feet, Sorrow and love flow mingled down! Did e'er such love and sorrow meet, Or thorns compose so rich a crown? Were the whole realm of nature mine, That were a present far too small; Love so amazing, so divine, Demands my soul, my life, my all."

> *When someone bears his reproach in this world,*
> *they are telling Jesus that his love is worth it and his love*
> *deserves all that they could possibly give.*

Mr. Watts knew that when a person truly studies the sacrifice that Jesus made for him, then his highest gain in this world no longer means anything to him. In comparison to the pure sacrificial love of Christ, all that we do is impure with selfish motivation in our hearts. All the accomplishments of our past, in view of the holy pure accomplishment of Calvary, only reveals how much our own are filled with pride and self-exaltation. From now on, I only desire to boast of the cross and the love of my Savior and King. Even if someone were to offer me a present of the world's approval, it could not compare to loving Jesus with all of my heart for what He has done for me. When one sees what love Christ has for him, he will seek only the approval of His beloved and not approval from the world. When someone bears his reproach in this world, they are telling Jesus that his love is worth it and his love deserves all that they could possibly give Him in return. Lastly, the Spirit of glory will rest upon any person that is suffering unjustly and carrying the reproach of their God and carrying shame for his holy name (see 1 Peter 4:14). We are commanded to go outside the camp, bearing his reproach (see Hebrews 13:13). The reproach that Jesus bore was the shame that his people have put upon the most beautiful, and the most pure heart. The Father unveiled the secret that had been hidden in his bosom for generations (see John 1:18) and the world and even God's chosen people mocked it, scorned it, hated it and destroyed it (Psalm 22:7-8). (For more on the subject, read the Author's book, "The Lamb's Heart").

When the camp is full of pride, self-centeredness, haughtiness, hatred, jealousy, and etc.; then the pure, lowly, lovely presence of God will not be welcome. God knows when He is wanted and he knows when He is not wanted. The fact that this sacred, pure heart, which lays down its life for others is not even desired, even in many that claim to love Him is what broke the heart of God (see Psalms 22, 68-69). Shame covered Jesus. It is written in Hebrews that Jesus *endured the cross, despising its shame"*. He despised the fact that the world considered the cross a shameful thing; while in truth the cross is the revelation of the Father's heart (see John 1:18). To suffer shame because you love the heart of Jesus is much greater than all the treasures the world can offer. This is one way to carry his reproach. David said that he only had one desire that he would always seek to fulfill. *"One thing have I desired, that will I seek, to be in the house of the Lord all the days of my life to behold the beauty of the Lord and to inquire in his temple"* (Psalm 27:4). What was the Beauty of the Lord that David was referring to? I believe it was when God unveiled his heart to his son David, and then David saw the most beautiful substance in all the multitude of galaxies.

Dear child of God, maybe you have felt abandoned by man and God, and maybe you thought you were just a broken, despised vessel. Father God is looking for broken, despised vessels to pour his pure, healing river of love into. When a person receives this pure, healing stream of love, they will find healing and then they will want to give it to others.

Will Jesus have to carry his shame all by himself or will you carry some of that shame also? There are many people that are grieving the Spirit of God every moment, but when someone carries his reproach, this somehow makes His pain a little less.

> *When a believer is wearing the mantle of humility (see Matthew 11:29), divine gentleness will flow through them into others.*

A HIDDEN SECRET IN THE INVISIBLE WORLD

"your gentleness has made me great." Psalm 18:35b (NKJV). In the invisible world, there are spiritual forces that are released when gentleness comes into someone. Pure love always flows through the gentleness of God. One of the fruits of the Spirit is gentleness (see Galatians 5:22). When a believer is wearing the mantle of humility (see Matthew 11:29), divine gentleness will flow through them into others.

If you will be a vessel for the gentleness of God unto your children, they will receive the favor of God into their lives and they will feel special even when they fail. When a child fails, it needs blessing and encouragement to get back up. When an individual shows gentleness to others they are carrying the reproach of Christ within them. A gentle, kind person will suffer shame from the world. When Jesus Christ hung almost naked, beaten, bloody and mocked on the cross for us, it is an honor to be mocked, scorned, and the shame we receive for His sake. The apostle Paul describes what a great honor it was to carry this reproach for Christ in the following words: *"I count all things but loss for the excellency of the knowledge of Christ Jesus my Lord: for whom I have suffered the loss of all things, and do count them but dung, that I may win Christ"* (Philippians 3:8).

When a parent, teacher or employer releases the gentleness of God to individuals that are under their supervision, these individuals will receive the glory of God upon them. When a person suffers shame for the name of Jesus Christ, the Spirit of glory is resting upon them, and the glory of God is being released through them to others (see 1 Peter 4:14). To live your life in the opposite spirit of pride that is in this world, is to live instead in the gentleness of the Lamb's heart. To live in the opposite spirit of the proud heart of men is to live in the gentleness of the heart of the Lamb. This will greatly please the Father. The Lamb is highly exalted and forever seated on the heavenly throne of his Father (Revelation 4, Philippians 2:7-11, Psalm 2, Revelation 5). Many teachers, have given those under them anger, criticism, hate, scorn, hard words, and etc. These innocent ones were denied gentleness and they in turn have incurred deep wounds and an inward sense of futility and hopelessness. When angry, hard words replace gentle kind words, these individuals will have to fight to become great in life (Psalm 18:35). Many wounded people are living out of the pain that was inflicted on them through hard, angry, or critical words.

To bear His reproach is to carry the shame, hate, and evil attitudes that the world has towards the Father; all the while knowing in my heart it is a lie and that the Father is so loving and perfect. As I carry His reproach in me, I can remit and retain the sins of others. Instead of holding a grudge or an offense towards others for something that they might have done to me, I can bear His reproach and release others from the evil that has them bound. I can now be a proclaimer of His kingdom, instead of proclaiming my right to be right. With my ego out of the way, and a clean heart, I can intercede for others and give my Lord his inheritance of the nations.

"I will declare the decree: The Lord hath said unto me, Thou art my Son; this day have I begotten thee. Ask of me, and I shall give thee the heathen for thine inheritance, and the uttermost parts of the earth for thy possession" (Psalm 2:7-8).

As a closing summary of this chapter, let's consider what Simon the Cyrene felt while he was carrying the cross for Jesus (Matthew 27:32). How he must have felt rejected, scorned and laughed at by the onlookers. Why would Simon have such feelings? It is for the same reason that Moses would have had all of those same feelings when he bore the reproach of Christ and esteemed it as greater riches than the treasures of Egypt (Hebrews 11:26). The feelings of hatred from others, rejection and scorn are the result of wanting to please God in your heart and in your life. Every child of God is called to carry the reproach of Christ (Hebrews 13:13). If it is understood that to carry the reproach of the Son of God in our daily life is a great honor, then it will not be seen as a negative, but instead as a great honor. Christ carried the reproach that was upon his father's lovely Self and we have the privilege to carry the reproach that is upon the beautiful, lovely face of Christ. This world is under the power of pride and selfishness and when a person chooses to walk in love and humility, a natural result of that choice is suffering shame for his holy name. To know the Father's heart is to understand how often the Spirit of God grieves over the pride of people that hate, lust, abuse, despise and dishonor others. May every born again believer take the privilege that God is offering them to carry His reproach and to bear his shame by doing what pleases the Father in your daily life, even as Jesus only did only what pleased.

CHAPTER 14
THE DEEP WOUND IN FATHER GOD'S HEART

I had great pain due to my big need of a father and mother's blessing, but for many, many years, I was not able to see that many of my problems were stemming from this relationship with my parents; until I finally received the truth that set me free. One day, after listening to many messages by Greg Violi, my fake world came crashing down on me. After I finally faced the truth of my deep pain, tremendous freedom came inside of my heart. Receiving a father's blessing greatly increased my love for God, for my father, and for everyone else. Now I have a deep inner certainty of Father God's love for me. Thank you God.

— *Elke S, Germany*

"And God saw that the wickedness of man was great in the earth, and that every imagination of the thoughts of his heart was only evil continually. And it repented the Lord that he had made man on the earth, and it grieved him at his heart."

(Genesis 6:5-6)

One day while reading the above scripture I cried and cried as I started to understand the wound that Father God carried inside of his heart. I struggled believing that mankind could have cut into the heart of the Father so deeply that he was sorry that He made us. God had a beautiful plan to have sons and daughters that would reveal who He was to the world. We were chosen in Him before the world began to be his adopted, beloved children. He pre-determined that He would have a family that was filled with his holy love (see Ephesians 1:4-6). God did not want to have robots that would automatically do what he desired for them, so he made all of his creation with the power of choice. One choice was to do the will of God. This choice would have resulted in every creature eating from the tree of life from God and revealing the image and likeness of God to others. Jesus said that unless we eat his flesh and drink his blood, we have no life in ourselves (see John 6:53). The second choice was to choose their own will and thereby reveal to others the image and nature of rebellion. Man chose the second choice and ever since the fall in Eden; men have thought and imagined evil in their hearts. God now saw that the thoughts and imaginations of their hearts were only evil continually. If man would have eaten from the other tree in the middle of the garden, called life, then man's thoughts and imaginations would have been love continually. When perfect love (God) saw that his creation was becoming evil, he became deeply wounded with the pain of rejection and abandonment. God was the first father to be abandoned by his son.

One day the Father said to his son, "Adam, where are you?" (see Genesis 3:9, Luke 3:38). Ever since Adam abandoned his father God, his children have been abandoning their children. *"Whatever a man sows this shall he also reap"* (Galatians 6:7b). All selfishness is a perverted form of love. True, pure love never seeks its own; but instead, it is always seeking to fill others with goodness, happiness and joy (see 1 John 4:12, 1 Corinthians 13:5b). After man chose his own selfish will; he suddenly found himself a vessel for every self-centered, independent desire which he wanted to fulfill. All the wars in the world have their origin in the selfish heart of men, which is to satisfy their lustful desires (see James 4:1). When the heart of man was filled with evil, something in the heart of God broke.

Many years later, men continued to break the heart of God and so God told Jeremiah, *"my people have forgotten me days without number"*

(Jeremiah 2:32). He also told Ezekiel one day that He was broken over the adulterous hearts of his people (see Ezekiel 6:9). Father God also told Hosea that it was Himself that stooped down to pick up his fallen children. It was God himself that loved his children, he drew them with cords of love, but his people are bent on turning away from him and backsliding (see Hosea 11:1-8).

> *Jesus declared that eternal life is to know the Father and the One he has sent into the world (see John 17:3).*

Jesus said that no person can truly know the father unless he (God) reveals himself to them (see Matthew 11:27). It grieved the heart of the Son that people did not understand that the Father was living his life inside of his Son (see John 14:7-10). Jesus declared that eternal life is to know the Father and the One he has sent into the world (see John 17:3). One day Jesus poured out his grieved heart, when he said, *"O righteous Father, the world hath not known thee; but I have known thee, and these have known that thou hast sent me."* (John 17:25).

Jesus fully understood his Father's heart and he also fully understood that the world really did not understand his father at all. One of the things that wounds Father God's heart is when millions of people attribute the evil that they experience as a direct result of God's activity. *"The foolishness of man perverts his way; and his heart rages against the Lord."* (Proverbs 19:3) *"The thief comes to steal, kill, and destroy"* (John 10:10a). The devil seeks only to hurt people. His entire heart is fixed upon causing harm and destruction to as many people as he can. So often though, the one that receives the blame for what the devil has done is the precious Heavenly father.

God gave his creation a sovereign choice to decide whether they would choose their own will or whether they would submit to the will of their Heavenly father. Lucifer, one-third of the angels, and mankind all chose their own selfish will, this put them under the power and dominion of sin. Sin is an entity that is the result of creation choosing their will in opposition to God's will (see Genesis 4:7). Anyone that chooses sin, becomes a slave to self-will. Sin is now their master and only Christ can free a person from the bondage of sin (see John 8:34). To know God's true heart of pure love and humility is a blessing. Father God has a very special love for widows, orphans, and needy people. *"He judged the cause of the poor and needy; then it was well with him: was not this to know me? saith the Lord"* (Jeremiah 22:6) (see also Jeremiah 9:24, James 1:27, Psalm 68:6).

Most people will relate to God the way that they related to their earthly father. If their earthly father was hard and demanding to them, they will see God the father as hard and demanding. If their earthly father did not have time for them because he was constantly busy with work, they will see their heavenly father as being too busy to spend time with them. If their earthly father was passive, they will expect God to be slow and passive and unfeeling. Some stories that Jesus told describes the way that many of God's children view God the Father. First, Jesus talks of the kingdom of heaven as a man that travels into a far off country who called his servants together and determined what they would receive. To the one servant he gave five talents, to one he gave two talents, and to one he gave one talent (see Matthew 25:14-27). The one that received the one talent said, *"Sir, I knew that thou art a hard man"*, *"and I was afraid"* (Matthew 25: 24b-25a). To this one, the master said, *"Thou slothful and wicked servant"* (Matthew 25: 26). This man, out of an inner attitude that the master was a hard man, was afraid and hid the master's talent. Many people that go to church also view God the Father as a hard man that is wanting to punish them as soon as they do something wrong.

The other story is the story of the prodigal son. The prodigal son went into sin, failure, made many mistakes, dishonored his father greatly, and by the standard of the law he should have been stoned. When the prodigal son returned his father embraced him, loved him, and wholeheartedly welcomed him back. He ran to kiss his son as soon as he beheld him coming from afar off. This father was so full of love and compassion that it caused him to run all the way to his son, he then fell upon his neck and kissed him. What a tremendous demonstration of pure love and mercy.

The other son, who actually lived with his kind, compassionate, and loving father had no understanding of what his own father was really like in his heart. He said with resentment to his father, *"you never gave me a kid [young goat] so that I could be happy with my friends"* (Luke 15:29b). This older son obeyed all of his father's commands, he never displeased his father, and he was a hard worker on his father's property. Yet, he thought his father did not want him to have a party and to have fun. How many Christians feel that deep down their Father God does not want them to have fun. Many children growing up experienced either never having fun or they lost their joy at an early age. After growing up in this way, they come to see God as a demanding taskmaster and not as a kind and joyful Father. The older son in the story was not happy and therefore was offended at his father's joy over the repentance of his brother (the sinner).

There are people that go to Church every week that could fit into this category with the older brother. They attend church, always try to obey God's commands, are hard workers for the kingdom, and are faithful in Christian activities. Even though they do all the right acceptable things on the outside; on the inside, they are sad, depressed and without the knowledge of their heavenly father's privileges for them. They are his children and all that He has belongs to them (see Luke 15:31). The Corinthian Christians were spiritually reconciled to God as born again believers in Christ, but they still needed a deeper reconciliation to their heavenly Father. *"Now then we are ambassadors for Christ, as though God did beseech you by us; we pray you in Christ's stead, be ye reconciled to God"* (2 Corinthians 5:20). It must deeply grieve the Father's heart to have so many of his children afraid of him and afraid of what he might be thinking about them.

John said, *"perfect love casts out fear"* (1 John 4:18) in the father's heart is the most perfect love ever. A kind father would feel sorrowful if his child was always afraid to ask him for a gift or a blessing? His heart would be yearning to release so many good things to his child, but no matter what he does for his child, what he does is always received with fear and suspicion. Jesus seemed to discern this fear and apprehension in people when he said,

"Ask, and it shall be given you; seek, and ye shall find; knock, and it shall be opened unto you: For every one that asketh receiveth; and he that seeketh findeth; and to him that knocketh it shall be opened. Or what man is there of you, whom if his son ask bread, will he give him a stone? Or if he ask a fish, will he give him a serpent? If ye then, being evil, know how to give good gifts unto your children, how much more shall your Father which is in heaven give good things to them that ask him?"

(Matt.7:7-11, Luke 11:10-13).

Here are some references to how greatly Father God loves to bless his children with everything that is good for them.

"He who did not spare his only son, but delivered him up for us all, how shall he not also with him freely give us all things."

Romans 8:32

"And in that day ye shall ask me nothing. Verily, verily I say to you, whatsoever ye shall ask the Father in my name, he will give it to you. Hitherto, ye have asked noting in my name, ask and ye shall receive, that your joy may be made full."

John 16:23-24

"Surely goodness and mercy shall follow me all the days of my life."

Psalm 23:6a

"Open thy mouth wide and I will fill it."

Psalm 81:10b

The Lord is gracious and full of compassion, slow to anger and of great mercy. The Lord is good to all and his tender mercies are over all his works."

Psalm 145:8-9

"For the Lord God is a sun and a shield; the LORD will give grace and glory; no good thing will he withhold from them that walk uprightly."

Psalm 84:11

If evil, earthly fathers can give good gifts to their children, how sad it is to think that our perfect, loving, unselfish heavenly Father will not graciously give us good gifts of love. New covenant believers are told to not, *"grieve the Holy Spirit"* (Ephesians 4:30a). What is your attitude, to God as your true Father that is in heaven? When you think of this great, almighty Being; who is also your very own father, what kind of thoughts come to your mind? What are your thoughts towards God as father? Do you desire to rather consider God only as Savior, Creator, Redeemer, or Judge? Do you prefer to only think upon the Son of God? Do you know intellectually that God is your father, but it gives you no feeling of affection and joy in your heart? Is the subject of the Fatherhood of God something that creates a deep fear inside of you? Does the word father create within you anger, fear or a deep sense of nothingness?

Maybe, your own earthly father abused you, abandoned you, controlled you, or rejected you. All of these things would have caused you to be uncovered in the spiritual world, leaving you open to the attacks of fear, bitterness, mental torment, rejection, self-pity, self-hatred, self-murder, depression, confusion, worthlessness, and unrighteous judgments. Your soul has been deeply wounded and your inner man has been greatly defiled if this was your experience as a child. Rejection always leaves a sting (hard feeling) and a wound inside if a person receives it. Father God yearned for your earthly father to cover you and to protect you (in the natural and in the spirit). God wanted desperately for your earthly father to love you, honor, and bless you. It was never his desire that your earthly father would do anything but bless, honor, and love you dearly! Father God suffers with every person that suffers in this world. In the midst of our own rejection, woundedness, and abuse; can we allow ourselves to feel and enter into the pain that the Father God has had within his heart ever since He created his children.

There is a special place inside of the heart of God for each person that is abused, abandoned, rejected, hated, or mistreated. In this special place is where the presence of God will abide and the wounded soul will experience the Spirit of glory and the loving, healing heart of the Father.

> *"For thus saith the high and lofty ONE that inhabits eternity, whose name is Holy; I dwell in the high and holy place, with him also that is of a contrite and humble spirit, to revive the spirit of the humble, and to revive the heart of the contrite ones."*
>
> (Isaiah 57:15)

The Father dwells in the very broken heart of the broken and abused ones because He understands what it feels like to be abandoned, broken, and rejected. The evil, wicked prince of darkness is constantly slandering and speaking evil of everyone, but the one whom he enjoys accusing and blaspheming the most is Father God. When this evil accuser is cast down, then the full manifestation of the kingdom and power of God will come forth.

> *"And I heard a voice in heaven, now is come salvation, and strength, and the kingdom of our God, and the power of our Christ: for the accuser of our brethren is cast down, which accused them before our God day and night."*
>
> (Revelation 12:10)

> *After God created Adam the accuser verbally attacked the Creator and accused him in the mind of Eve, "God doth know that in the*

day ye eat thereof, then your eyes shall be opened, and ye shall be as gods, knowing good and evil"

(Genesis 3:5).

> *God only speaks the truth, for he is the truth and he can never tell a lie.*

Most of the negative, bad thoughts that are towards God in the world today are a direct result of the accuser. He, the devil, is slandering and accusing Father God in the minds and hearts of all mankind. Jesus said, *"...there is no truth in him. When he speaks a lie, he speaks of his own: For he is a liar, and the father of it"* (John 8:44b). The devil is the father of all lies. He does not speak the truth. His very nature is to tell a lie or to always distort the truth. On the other hand, God only speaks the truth, for he is the truth and he can never tell a lie. Millions of people have received evil lies regarding Father God, they unfortunately believe that God is a father who does not take care of his children.

The negative and hateful attitude of this world, against Father God, is what Jesus carried to the cross. Jesus felt in his soul and carried all the shame, reproach, lies, and hate against his father in his body when he hung on the cross. His soul was literally poured out unto death. It was this evil that broke the heart of Jesus and caused him to be filled with heaviness. Since he was made sin, he took upon himself all of our defilements, sicknesses, curses, rebellion and evil; so that he could destroy it and totally break all of its power over the human race at the cross. He never once sinned, but the Father made him to be Sin for us. Through death, he destroyed the power of death and the power of the devil.

"Because of thy sake I have borne reproach; shame has covered my face"
(Psalm 69:7).

"For the zeal of thine house has eaten me up, and the reproaches of them that reproached thee are fallen upon me"
(Psalm 69:9).

"Reproach has broken my heart; and I am full of heaviness: and I looked for some to take pity, but there was none; and for comforters, but I found none"

(Psalm 69:20).

The Son of God carried the Father's shame and dishonor. He felt the full measure of reproach and dishonor that the world has toward the Father. Jesus Christ was the perfect mediator between God and man. He drank the full measure of the cup of wrath that was to be poured out on men for their rebellion and sin. He became the perfect substitute for us so that we can be redeemed through his death on the cross. He also bore the full measure of the reproach of a rejected and hated God into his very bosom. He took the wrath that man deserved. He felt the reproach and shame of God, in his body, because he chose to bear the cross, he has now reconciled God with man.

The heart of the Father has been hated for thousands of years until this very day, Jesus is still rejected and despised of men. Isaiah 53:3 says: *"He is despised and rejected of men; a man of sorrows, and acquainted with grief; and we hid as it were our faces from Him; he was despised, and we esteemed him not."*

Jesus is despised by men to this day, we are called to carry his reproach. Just like Jesus bore the shame and reproach of his father's wounded heart, even so we are now to carry his wounded heart.

"Who now rejoice in my sufferings for you, and fill up that which is lacking of the afflictions of Christ in my flesh for his body's sake, which is the church"

(Colossians 1:24).

"Let us go forth therefore unto HIM without the camp, bearing his reproach"

(Hebrews 13:13).

"And to him they agreed: and when they had called the apostles, and beaten them, they commanded that they should not speak in

the name of Jesus, and let them go. And they departed from the presence of the council, rejoicing that they were counted worthy to suffer shame for his name"

(Acts 5:40-41).

Why is the Father's heart so wounded? He desired His greatest creation, being man, to rule and to reign over all His universe. Unfortunately, he forfeited his regal right to the evil one after he sinned. Father still desires His sons and daughters to rule and represent who He is in this universe, but His creation prefers another ruler. This other ruler has a heart that is full of everything the Father hates and this is why John says "If we love the world, the love of the Father is not in us." (see 1 John 2:15b) This world is under an evil prince (see Ephesians 2:2; 2 Corinthians 4:4; 1 John 5:19).

This world system has created a false manhood that totally misrepresents the Fatherhood of God and glorifies the manhood of Esau, of which God said *"Esau I have hated"* (Malachi 1:3). Men in today's world are encouraged to be rebellious to divine authority and not submit to a ruler over them, to be independent, like Esau. He was healthy, assertive, and he was an outdoorsman. Esau was a good hunter, strong and worldly. He had a large family, was wealthy, was a good leader, and he lived for the present moment. There was just one major problem with Esau. He was a profane, godless man that had no concern for godliness and spiritual things. This is the type of man that is highly esteemed in today's cultures. But, there is one true man, by which the Father will judge all men. *"Because he hath appointed a day, in the which he will judge the world in righteousness by that man whom he hath ordained; whereof he hath given assurance unto all men, in that he hath raised him from the dead"* (Acts 17:31).

These two words appointed and ordained have the following meanings:

ordained, Strong's G2476 – histēmi- to cause or make to stand, to place, put, set, to bid to stand by, [set up].

Appointed, Strong's G3724 – horizon- to mark out the boundaries or limits (of any place or thing), to determine, appoint, that which has been determined, acc. to appointment, decree.

True manhood according to the standard of heaven has been fully and totally demonstrated by the man Christ Jesus.

"For there is one God, and one mediator between God and men, the man Christ Jesus" (1 Timothy 2:5).

> *"Ye men of Israel, hear these words; Jesus of Nazareth, a man approved of God among you by miracles and wonders and signs, which God did by him in the midst of you, as ye yourselves also know"*
>
> (Acts 2:22).

Jesus was a complete living example of what Father God always intended a man in his own image to look like.

Jesus was a complete living example of what Father God always intended a man in his own image to look like. Jesus always demonstrated manhood outwardly through obedience to God's will, and inwardly, through humility of heart towards all man. His daily life consisted of always loving, servitude, and making himself nothing in the eyes of others (see Philippians 2:7-8).

> *"No man hath seen God at any time; the only begotten Son, which is in the bosom of the Father, he hath declared him"*
>
> (John 1:18).

Jesus reveals to all people what is in the depths of his Father's heart (the bosom). The heart and mind of God is seen clearly in the outward life of the Son. The Father reached deep inside of his heart and he took out his greatest treasure, his beloved Son and offered him to the world to behold and adore. The world however in all of its ugliness, depravity, and pride caused them to fail in seeing the exquisite beauty of the Son. Instead of adoring him, they hated him, despised him, and finally crucified him. This was especially true with the religious leaders at this time, they could not tolerate such purity and holiness in a human body. His purity exposed their impurity. His humility exposed their pride and arrogance. His love exposed their religious hate. His mercy and kindness totally unveiled their hearts of legalistic intolerance and wrath. Their dark hearts were uncovered by his very presence and the purity of his words (see John 15:22). For the religious leaders to hate Jesus, they had to also hate the Father, because Jesus was the representation of the Father in the flesh.

> *"Who being the brightness of his glory, and the express image of his person"*
>
> (Hebrews 1:3a).

Loving this world system and its ways and loving what it represents, is to hate what the Father represents.

> *"Ye adulterers and adulteresses, know ye not that the friendship of the world is hatred to God? Whosoever therefore will be a friend of the world is the enemy of God".*
>
> (James 4:4)

The great apostle John also said, *"Love not the world, neither the things that are in the world; if any man love the world, the love of the Father is not in him"* (1 John 2:16). The world system in its evil pride has manufactured a father that can control and dominate his children (even in a religious or Christian sense), and call it the "norm". This father can abuse, scream, abandon, ignore his responsibility, live in pride, and reject the fear of God in his own life.

Many promises and blessings of being a man that fears God are given in Psalm 112, but still this worldly type of man will wonder why his life has not brought blessings and fulfillment to his family and children.

"Praise ye the Lord. Blessed is the man that feareth the Lord and delighteth greatly in his commandments. His seed shall be mighty upon earth: the generation of the upright shall be blessed. Wealth and riches shall be in his house: and his righteousness endureth forever. Unto the upright there arrives light in the darkness: he is gracious, and full of compassion, and righteous. A good man sheweth favor and lendeth: he will guide his affairs with discretion. Surely he shall not be moved forever: the righteous shall be in everlasting remembrance. He shall not be afraid of evil tidings: his heart is fixed, trusting the Lord"

(Psalm 112:1-7).

The world has fallen so short of the will of God; especially in his heart of lowly, pure love. God considers some of his faith-filled, loving servants as those whom this world is not worthy of their very presence.

"Of whom the world was not worthy"
(Hebrews 11:38a).

These people whom the Father said the world was not worthy of their presence lived their lives in faith, trusting in the invisible God by loving and doing his will with total allegiance to his purposes on earth. Many of these persecuted saints, that have gone before us are now in the cloud of witnesses that surrounds us and encourages us to run this race and win the prize with our eyes fixed only on Jesus (see Hebrews 12:1-2).

At this very hour, God the Holy Spirit is raising up mighty men that will follow their leader David (Jesus) into the end-time battle and triumphantly declare and reveal His kingdom. David had many mighty men that were joined with him against the unrighteous rule of King Saul, knowing that the rule of Saul (flesh) was getting weaker and weaker, but the rule of David (Spirit) was getting stronger and stronger (see 2 Samuel 3:1). God is still looking for these mighty men that will stand in the gap for the land and fill in the breaches (see 2 Samuel 10:7; 16:6; 23:8-9, 16-17, 22). The rule of David is very important because there is only ONE who can sit on the throne of his father David and he is the Son of David. David has great significance in Biblical history and through the Messiah His kingdom will rule forever. There is a spirit of Jonathan today that wants to unite the kingdom of Saul with the kingdom of David. This spirit is very nice on the outside, but the person allowing it to operate in them is lacking understanding in the purposes of God. Zadok represents the faithful priesthood of this day that will only stand uncompromisingly with the true King and His reign.

The sons of Zadok represent a holy priesthood of mighty men that are rising up now to stand for the righteous reign of David on the earth. The word Zadok itself means righteous and Melchizedek means the king of righteousness. Today, the priestly/kingly order of Melchizedek is coming forth on earth to reveal the eternal Word in His majestic glory. This is a heavenly priesthood that is called to reveal the heavenly realm in character, dominion, and glory.

> "But Zadok the priest, and Benaiah the son of Jehoiada, and Nathan the prophet, and Shim, and Rei, and the mighty men which belonged to David were not with Adonijah"
>
> (1 Kings 1:8-9).

> "And I sought for a man amongst them that should make up the hedge, and stand in the gap before me for the land, that I should not destroy it: but I found none"
>
> (Ezekiel 22:30).

Adonijah, in the natural world, should have been the king after David, but God's choice was clearly Solomon (1 Kings 1:30). Zadok always stood with the righteous reign of David and God said that only the sons of Zadok could minister to him.

"But the priests the Levites, the sons of Zadok, that kept the charge of my sanctuary when the children of Israel went astray from me, they shall come near to me to minister unto me, and they shall stand before me"

(Ezekiel 44:15a).

The sons of Zadok represent the order of Melchizedek, which is a heavenly priesthood of the Lamb that is now coming forth in great authority and power to execute the righteous reign of Christ and his kingdom. It is time to represent the heavenly man and to stop representing the man of this earth, that man is earthly-minded. (see Matthew 16:23)

"The first man [was] from out of earth, made of dust (earthly-minded); the second Man [is] the Lord from out of heaven. Now those who are made of the dust are like him who was first made of the dust (earthly-minded); and as is [the Man] from heaven, so also [are those] who are of heaven (heavenly-minded). And just as we have borne the image [of the man] of dust, so shall we and so [a] let us also bear the image [of the Man] of heaven."

(1 Corinthians 15:47-49 Amplified Bible, Classic Edition [AMPC]).

A true apostle will bear the image of the heavenly man Christ Jesus and he will suffer the reproach of Christ from the world.

"For I think that God hath set forth us the apostles last, as it were appointed to death: for we are made a spectacle unto the world, and to angels, and to men. We are fools for Christ's sake, but ye are wise in Christ; we are weak, but ye are strong; ye are honorable, but we are despised. Even unto this present hour we both hunger, and thirst, and are naked, and are buffeted, and have no certain dwelling place; and labor, working with our own hands: being reviled, we bless; being persecuted, we suffer it: Being defamed, we entreat: we are made as the filth of the world, and are the off scouring of all

*things unto this day. I write not these things to shame you, but as my
beloved sons I warn you. For though ye have ten thousand instructors
in Christ, yet have ye not many fathers: for in Christ Jesus I have
begotten you through the gospel"*

(1 Corinthians 4:9-15).

A spiritual father, like the apostle Paul, will carry the shame and
reproach of Christ in this world. Also, Moses esteemed the reproach
of Christ as greater riches than all of the treasures of Egypt (Hebrews
11:26).

What would you choose? Maybe your father abandoned or abused
you and he never fulfilled his purpose on this earth as a godly man and
father to you. Will you allow your experience with your earthly father
to influence your relationship with your Heavenly Father? Will you
choose to follow in his footsteps or will you humble yourself and ask
the Holy Spirit to make you a man after God's own heart like David?
Will you allow the kingdom of God the Father to come over you right
now and superimpose itself over any other kingdom that has been
working in you?

Prayer:

*Right now, in the name of Jesus Christ, receive the blessing of God upon
you to suffer for hIs name sake. Receive healing my dear brother and sister,
from the wounds of rejection, pain, and trauma; especially the trauma
of being hated for wanting to please God with your life. Be healed and
restored now to love the Father and carry the reproach of His heart in this
world.*

CHAPTER 15

THE TRUE LIGHT OF ALL MEN

I started translating the Finding Father book into German when my legs started swelling and my heart rate went up. I received Psalm 71: 6 telling me that God the father was at my birth, delivering me out of my mother's womb. I wept and wept and didn't even know why. I tried to get up and fell down with a sharp pain in my hip and cried even more. I could suddenly see how my heavenly father had always been there, lovingly, and how Satan had fabricated the lie through my earthly father's rejection, that father God had rejected me also.

Then, as the day unfolded, I heard two testimonies of children that were set free from spirits of fear of water. Then I mentioned the impact of the text in the morning and how the Father had highlighted the pregnancy. My mother had been hospitalized during it and was made to drink just tiny amounts of water because she retained so much water. Suddenly Pastor Greg stood up and held my hand and started praying. I was instantly released from a spirit called fear of having too much water that my mum received when doctors told her not to drink too much water because of the water retention.

It was the Father himself coming through His servant to deliver his daughter. After the lie was broken off me, that he wasn't there at my birth and I was rejected, the heavenly Father could freely come and give me the gift of freely receiving from him. I was set free of the fear of too much water. For a whole day I felt like waking up from a long heavy dream. My body felt so light. I enjoyed drinking water instead of forcing myself to drink it. Over the following two days my heart rate returned to normal, my legs stopped swelling and my body stopped retaining water.

But what makes me happiest is to experience the goodness of the Father like never before, his loving-kindness and his gentleness. I couldn't stop crying about his compassion and love. I want others to come back to the Father and to be released from the lies of the evil one.

– Ruth S. Germany

I cannot remember my earthly father really paying attention to what I was saying or giving me the feeling that my words were of any value to him. When I received the father's blessing I heard my heavenly father very clearly: My son, I listen to every word you say and every word you say is of great value to me. These words healed a deep pain within me, a pain I did not even know I had.

– Harald F, Germany

God is light and there is no darkness in Him, therefore for a man to be a true man he must walk in the light. As he walks in light, he will reveal what a true man looks like to others. In this chapter we will discuss true manhood and true light. The manhood of this world derives its title from the standards of this worldly system. Therefore, since the god of this worldly system is filled with pride, then the men that follow his standard cannot possibly reveal a true man. Instead this worldly man will live in his false self with a subconscious need to find himself. He is constantly trying to discover why he is here on earth and how to find satisfaction in life. When we look into the face of Jesus Christ, we are clearly beholding the countenance of a true man in which the Father is clearly seen. His standards can all be summarized in one definitive word; unselfishness. It is the unselfish nature of His heart that causes him to be a vessel for pure love. As soon as a man discovers that an unselfish heart is the key to true manhood, then he is faced with some serious choices in life. Firstly, am I willing to look foolish in the eyes of the world while I demonstrate the heart of the Father? Secondly, Do I really see the value of being a leader that shines the light of pure love?

We must ask ourselves, are we willing to embrace with joy His reproach in us?

"But what things were gain to me, those I counted loss for Christ. Yea doubtless, and I count all things but loss for the excellency of the knowledge of Christ Jesus my Lord: for whom I have suffered the loss of all things, and do count them but dung, that I may win Christ, and be found in him, not having mine own righteousness, which is of the law, but that which is through the faith of Christ, the righteousness which is of God by faith: That I may know him, and the power of his resurrection, and the fellowship of his sufferings, being made conformable unto his death; if by any means I might attain unto the resurrection of the dead. Not as though I had already attained, either were already perfect: but I follow after, if that I may apprehend that for which also I am apprehended of Christ Jesus. Brethren, I count not myself to have apprehended: but this one thing I do, forgetting those things which are behind, and reaching forth unto those things which are before, I press toward the mark for the prize of the high calling of God in Christ Jesus"

(Philippians 3:7-14).

The reproach that Christ carried was how he was treated by mankind and especially by his own people. He was perfect in every way, but others treated him as a curse, Beelzebub, the prince of devils, sin, and even as if he was an unclean animal. He gladly made himself nothing in the eyes of others. Even though the most astounding miracles took place, which could have vindicated his ministry; he said, "tell no man". He willingly died on a tree, which identified him as someone that was cursed by God. He died outside the camp, because to die inside the camp would have defiled and polluted the camp. Just as a leper was not allowed to be inside the camp, because his leprosy would have made the entire camp unclean, so was it in the same way with Jesus. Jesus died as a leper, a worm, and not even treated with dignity as a man.

"But I am a worm, and no man; a reproach of men, and despised of the people. All they that see me laugh me to scorn: they shoot out the lip, they shake the head, saying, He trusted on the Lord that he

would deliver him: let him deliver him, seeing he delighted in him. But thou art he that took me out of the womb: thou didst make me hope when I was upon my mother's breasts. I was cast upon thee from the womb: thou art my God from my mother's belly. Be not far from me; for trouble is near; for there is none to help. Many bulls have compassed me: strong bulls of Bashan have beset me round. They gaped upon me with their mouths, as a ravening and a roaring lion. I am poured out like water, and all my bones are out of joint: my heart is like wax; it is melted in the midst of my bowels. My strength is dried up like a potsherd; and my tongue cleaved to my jaws; and thou hast brought me into the dust of death. For dogs have compassed me: the assembly of the wicked have enclosed me: they pierced my hands and feet. I may tell all my bones: they look and stare upon me. They part my garments among them, and cast lots upon my vesture. But be not thou far from me, o Lord: o my strength, haste thee to help me. Deliver my soul from the sword; my darling from the power of the dog. Save me from the lion's mouth: for thou hast heard me from the horns of the unicorns. I will declare thy name unto my brethren: in the midst of the congregation will I praise thee. Ye that fear the Lord, praise him; all ye the seed of Jacob, glorify him; and fear him, all ye the seed of Israel. For he hath not despised nor abhorred the affliction of the afflicted; neither hath he hid his face from him; but when he cried unto him, he heard. My praise shall be of thee in the great congregation: I will pay my vows before them that fear him. The meek shall eat and be satisfied: they shall praise the Lord that seek him: your heart shall live forever"

(Psalm 22:6-26).

Jesus's worldly brothers told him, go show thyself to the people, because no one that is seeking a following, will do these things in secret, like this.

"His brethren therefore said unto him, depart hence, and go into Judaea, that thy disciples also may see the works that thou doeth.

For there is no man that doeth anything in secret, and he himself seeketh to be known openly. If thou do these things, shew thyself to the world"

(John 7:3-4).

"Then Jesus said unto them, my time is not yet come: but your time is always ready. The world cannot hate you; but me it hateth, because I testify of it, that the works thereof are evil"

(John 7:6-7).

Jesus, the true man, never sought others to follow him, but instead, he only sought to glorify His Father in heaven and to do His will on earth. Many worldly men will seek to be honored and esteemed by others without considering how God views them. Jesus only longed to bring pleasure to the heart of his Father.

"I receive not honor from men. But I know you, that ye have not the love of God in you. I am come in my Father's name, and ye receive me not: if another shall come in his own name, him ye will receive. How can ye believe, which receive honour one of another, and seek not the honor that cometh from God only?"

(John 5:41-44).

"Nevertheless among the chief rulers also many believed on him; but because of the Pharisees they did not confess him, lest they should be put out of the synagogue: For they loved the praise of men more than the praise of God"

(John 12:42-43).

"I have glorified thee on the earth: I have finished the work which thou gavest me to do"

(John 17:4).

Please ask yourself, am I willing and wanting to let this pure and holy attitude of heart to be inside of me; even as my Lord and Master had it inside of him.

"Ye call me Master and Lord: and ye say well; for so I am. If I then, your Lord and Master, have washed your feet; ye also ought to wash one another's feet. For I have given you an example, that ye should do as I have done to you. Verily, verily, I say unto you, the servant is not greater than his lord; neither he that is sent greater than he that sent him"

(John 13:13-17).

"Let this mind be in you, which was also in Christ Jesus: who, being in the form of God, thought it not robbery to be equal with God: But made himself of no reputation, and took upon him the form of a servant, and was made in the likeness of men: And being found in fashion as a man, he humbled himself, and became obedient unto death, even the death of the cross. Wherefore God also hath highly exalted him, and given him a name which is above every name"

(Philippians 2:5-9).

> *The system of this world is in direct opposition to the ways of the heavenly kingdom. Therefore, what is highly esteemed by this world is an abomination in the eyes of God.*

"For that which is highly esteemed among men is abomination in the sight of God"

(Luke 16:15b).

The religious system as a whole is under the power of image and how it appears in the eyes of others, while the Kingdom of God is under the power of an endless life. The one system is based on law, while the other system is based on life, which in its truest essence is pure love! The one system has inner motives that are seeking to be exalted in the eyes of others; while the other system is seeking only to be pleasing in the eyes of the Maker.

"And whatsoever ye do in word or deed, do all in the name of the Lord Jesus, giving thanks to God and the Father by him. Wives,

submit yourselves unto your own husbands, as it is fit in the Lord. Husbands, love your wives, and be not bitter against them. Children, obey your parents in all things: for this is well pleasing unto the Lord. Fathers, provoke not your children to anger, lest they be discouraged. Servants, obey in all things your masters according to the flesh; not with eye service, as men pleasers; but in singleness of heart, fearing God: and whatsoever ye do, do it heartily, as to the Lord, and not unto men; knowing that of the Lord ye shall receive the reward of the inheritance: for ye serve the Lord Christ"

(Colossians 3:17-24).

> *The Father has determined that He has a set day, the day in which all mankind will be judged in the light of the one true man, which He has ordained to be the standard of all men.*

"And the times of this ignorance God winked at; but now commandeth all men everywhere to repent: Because he hath appointed a day, in the which he will judge the world in righteousness by that man whom he hath ordained; whereof he hath given assurance unto all men, in that he hath raised him from the dead"

(Acts 17:30-31).

This standard is Jesus Christ. The standard is not Gandhi, Martin Luther, or John Wesley. There is only one standard and His name is Jesus Christ and He is the true light that enlightens every man.

"And this is the condemnation, that light is come into the world, and men loved darkness rather than light, because their deeds were evil. For every one that doeth evil hateth the light, neither cometh to the light, lest his deeds should be reproved. But he that doeth truth cometh to the light, that his deeds may be made manifest, that they are wrought in God"

(John 3:19-21).

"The same came for a witness, to bear witness of the Light that all men through him might believe. He was not that Light, but was sent to bear witness of that Light. That was the true Light, which lighteth every man that cometh into the world. He was in the world, and the world was made by him, and the world knew him not"

(John 1:7-10).

Christ the standard, who is the true light and true man, will expose all the hidden desires within men's hearts that are impure and selfish. Therefore there is not one impure, selfish motive within the heart of Jesus. His very Presence in a room exposes all the darkness of evil that is buried in the heart of an individual. The condemnation of the world is that the world does not want truth to expose its hidden corruption. A worldly person will not come to the light because their hidden, evil thoughts will be revealed. There is another group of individuals that love the truth and come to the light so that their deeds will be made manifest whether they were accomplished or wrought in God or in self (see John 3:21).

David knew the difference between pure, holy light and impure deceptive light. He lived his life so that his thoughts, motives, and attitudes would please God. No matter what he was doing, whether watching sheep, running an errand for his father, or killing a giant it was all done to reveal how great his God was and to show what a true heart of worship looks like. He said in Psalms, *"in thy light shall we see light"* (Psalms 36:9b). *"All men at his very best state is vanity"*, (Psalm 39:6b). The writer of Ecclesiastes, the wisest man on earth, writes:

"I said in mine heart concerning the estate of the sons of men, that God might manifest them, and that they might see that they themselves are beasts"

(Ecclesiastes 3:18).

Why did the religious leaders of Jesus's day have so much hatred for this holy man in their midst? In their pride they assumed what they were seeing was the truth, but the truth they thought they were seeing, was only through deceptive light.

> "And Jesus said, for judgment I am come into this world, that they which see not might see; and that they which see might be made blind. And some of the Pharisees which were with him heard these words, and said unto him, Are we blind also? Jesus said unto them, if ye were blind, ye should have no sin: but now ye say, We see; therefore your sin remaineth"
>
> (John 9:39-41).

The light of the religious leaders could easily reveal the sinful condition of the harlots, murderers, and drunkards. The light that Jesus walked in was so bright that it easily could expose the hidden motives and thoughts of the hearts. No person can or will be justified in the light of the holiness of Almighty God. Religion has told people that they can be accepted in God's sight based on their own performances. Unfortunately, false religious light deceives all men into believing that they are not bad sinners; therefore they will be accepted with God. The light that they were operating in could only show what was on the outside and it had no power to reveal what was in the heart. God always looks at our heart and man always looks at the outward appearance.

> "But the Lord said unto Samuel, look not on his countenance, or on the height of his stature; because I have refused him: for the Lord seeth not as man seeth; for man looketh on the outward appearance, but the Lord looketh on the heart"
>
> (1 Samuel 16:7).

> "Now we know that what things so ever the law saith, it saith to them who are under the law: that every mouth may be stopped, and

the entire world may become guilty before God. Therefore by the deeds of the law there shall no flesh be justified in his sight: for by the law is the knowledge of sin"

(Romans 3:19-20).

> *If I am using my own light as my own standard to make decisions regarding my spiritual state, then I am certainly going to be deceived.*

Isaiah said that all of our *"righteousnesses are as filthy rags"* in God's sight (see Isaiah 64:6). Jesus said take heed that the light that is in thee be not darkness (see Luke 11:35). If I am using my own light as my own standard to make decisions regarding my spiritual state, then I am certainly going to be deceived. If I am willing to come into His pure light and to let His pure motives of love be my judge, then I will certainly discover the areas of darkness that have been hidden within my heart. The lamp of the body is the eye, therefore, the motive of my heart (what my eyes are focused on) will determine how much light is shining out of my eyes. If my eye is single and I only have one desire and one focus, which is to please God in all things, then my entire body will be full of light (see Luke 11:34).

This is how Jesus lived his entire life on earth. It was written of him that he desired to do His father's will. *"Then said I, Lo, I come: in the volume of the book it is written of me, I delight to do thy will, O my God: yea, thy law is within my heart"* (Psalm 40:7-8). Within the very depths of his heart, was the eternal, pure law of love. Love never seeks its own. Not for one moment will the pure love of God have any selfish desires in it. This means that every word that Jesus spoke had only one desire and that was to bring his listeners deeper into the love of His Father.

Over the centuries, religion has taught multitudes to live by the "love of the law" instead of living by the "law of love". The law has only been capable of telling us when our actions are right or wrong.

For example when there is a speeding law, it notifies you of the speed limit, the limit lets you know as to whether your actions were right or wrong. Paul said that by the knowledge of law, he was found to be righteous and blameless (see Philippians 3:6). Law will deal with rebellious behavior coming forth from an individual; but the pure love of God seen in the person of Jesus will expose the hidden secrets of my heart as to every motive.

"For God shall bring every work into judgment, with every secret thing, whether it be good, or whether it be evil"

(Ecclesiastes 12:14).

> *Ask yourself what does this perfect, true light look like in a body.*

This is perfectly demonstrated in the person of Jesus Christ while he was on earth. A life lived to the glory of God. Jesus did only that which pleased His Father through his speech, by his actions, and through his thoughts. His speech always released the Spirit of God and the very life of God (see John 6:63). Jesus never sought glory from men. He always did what pleased the Father, even if others hated him for doing it. He purposely made himself appear as a servant or slave; He never sought people's applause to anything that he did. He shunned men's approval in his life in order to be free from the bondage of the fear of man, which always brings a snare.

> *He purposely made himself appear as a servant or slave; He never sought people's applause to anything that he did.*

"The fear of man bringeth a snare: but whoso putteth his trust in the Lord shall be safe"

(Proverbs 29:25).

Obedience characterized his daily life, for there was no trace of rebellion in him. He never reacted to the evil speech of others and their attempts to trick him and trap him. He saw how people hated him and discerned it as hatred towards His Father. This same hatred was also against what His Father represented to the people. Since Jesus came to fully reveal what was inside of his Father, when he washed his disciples feet and touched the lepers; this revealed what his Father was thinking about humanity. When people had such angry reactions to Jesus Christ they were exposing the true attitudes of their hearts concerning God's lowly heart. He said, if I came in another man's name instead of in my Father's name, then you would receive me (see John 5:43). He allowed people to do many things against him such as: falsely accuse, slander, oppose, reject, hate, abuse, lie about him, spit on him, mock him, destroy his reputation, curse him, misunderstand him, blaspheme him, misrepresent him and abandon him.

Jesus suffered agonizing torment while being utterly forsaken by everyone and dying while many were watching, laughing, and cursing him, and mutilating his body so bad that he could barely be recognized as a human (see Isaiah 52:14). Throughout his life Jesus was considered by many including his own family members, as a bastard, deceiver, unclean man, false prophet, blasphemer, a cult leader, troublemaker, fake, worthy of death, and etc. What was the reason that Jesus went through all of this treatment, suffering, pain, and even death? Why? To reveal His Father's heart to all of creation and to demonstrate father's love to them. His Father was in the very center of all that Jesus ever did. This pure light perfectly revealed the holiness of God, because there was no darkness to defile the expression of God's holiness (see John 14:30). This pure light will deeply satisfy the heart of God, because it can now reveal the image of God to the world.

From the very beginning of the world, God desired to make man in his own image and likeness (see Genesis 1:26). After man fell from the true image of God, he descended into a false self that reveals a distorted image of who God is. When the Word became flesh and dwelt amongst men, he came as the true light that enlightens every man. After Adam fell, he now gave birth to a son in his own image and likeness.

"This is the book of the generations of Adam. In the day that God created man, in the likeness of God made he him; male and female created he them; and blessed them, and called their name Adam, in the day when they were created. And Adam lived an hundred and thirty years, and begat a son in his own likeness, after his image; and called his name Seth"

(Genesis 5:1-3).

> *The question that we should all ask ourselves is: Do I want to reveal my own corrupted, impure image to others or do I want to reveal the pure image of my Creator to others?*

Adam started having children in his own corrupted image that was defiled with a false image and that revealed a false god to the world. This false representation of our Creator reveals a selfish person that is concerned only with himself, how others relate to him, and how his own needs can be met through others. The question that we should all ask ourselves is: Do I want to reveal my own corrupted, impure image to others or do I want to reveal the pure image of my Creator to others? Only when we do not care about how others see us, can we start to focus on how others see God's image in us. When we lose our need to maintain our own defiled image, then we can allow the Holy Spirit to reveal the very image of Christ though us while we bear his reproach in our body and soul.

CHAPTER 16

THE TRUE SELF IS SHINING FORTH AND THE NEW DAY IS DAWNING

I received a father's blessing from Greg Violi 9 months ago and since then my life has changed. I am coming alive. I have the feeling of "being" instead of "not-being." I am starting to enjoy life. I can just be, without having to justify my existence.

— Andreea F, South Germany

"But when that which is perfect is come, then that which is in part shall be done away. When I was a child, I spoke as a child, I understood as a child, I thought as a child. But when I became a man, I put away childish things"

(1 Corinthians 13:10-11).

I trust that you have seen that which is perfect in the face of Jesus Christ. When we look deeply into his glorious face, we can see the perfect plan of the Father for all of his creation.

As we step into the true self and choose to put on the Lord Jesus, we make ourselves ready to be healed of all the childish things such as: wounds, traumas, memories, thought patterns, and etc. These childish things have kept us short of the perfect and wonderful purpose which Father God had planned for us. Our future is not bound, blocked, or hindered because of what has happened to us in our past. Our future depends on one thing: Our heart attitude toward our loving, redemptive heavenly Father! The Father has determined that a true king and priest is one that is lowly. The new order of the kingdom of priests is: Exalt him that is low and abase him that is high.

"And whosoever shall exalt himself shall be abased; and he that shall humble himself shall be exalted"

(Matthew 23:12).

> *Therefore, as we close this book, we humble ourselves under the mighty hand of God so that He may lift us up in due time (see 1 Peter 5:6).*

God chooses the lowly, unaffirmed, and despised ones to be Kings in his Kingdom. Their problem is often about seeing their true selves in the true light of His calling. It is His word that calls them into being the prince and king that they become. However they are many times stuck in the mud and quicksand of living in an ash heap in their mind. Instead of seeing themselves as a rightful heir to the throne in Christ, they still are weighed down under the mindset of being a poor beggar unworthy of any good thing.

JACOB

"And he said, Thy name shall be called no more Jacob, but Israel: for as a prince hast thou power with God and with men, and hast prevailed"

(Genesis 32:28).

Jacob said to Pharaoh, *"The years of my journey through life are 130. My years have been few and hard (Troublesome and difficult). They aren't as many as the years of my father and grandfather before me"* (Genesis 47:9). Jacob did not see himself as a prince with his God, instead he saw himself as a rejected boy, who spent much time with his mother. It is the role of a father to affirm his children; the mother does not have the ability to affirm her children's gender. Isaac preferred Esau over his brother Jacob and it was always Jacob's mother that was intervening and helping Jacob to make decisions in his life. Isaac apparently did not give Jacob the affirmation that he needed in his life. Jacob spent many years in depression and sorrow and it was only when he saw the wagons that Joseph sent to fetch him out of his land that his inner man was revived.

> *"And told him, saying, Joseph is yet alive, and he is governor over all the land of Egypt. And Jacob's heart fainted, for he believed them not. And they told him all the words of Joseph, which he had said unto them: and when he saw the wagons which Joseph had sent to carry him, the spirit of Jacob their father revived: And Israel said, It is enough; Joseph my son is yet alive: I will go and see him before I die"*
> (Genesis 45:26-28).

When he saw the wagons, his spirit revived. That means that for all the years that Joseph was not with his father, his spirit was in a state of depression and only when he saw the wagons, he was revived (encouraged). The wagons represent the promises of God in our life. Many of God's children live in sadness because they are waiting for the promises of God to be fulfilled.

MOSES

The next Prince in God's sight was Moses. Moses was brought up in a royal palace, where he would learn the ways of royalty as he matured. *"And he said, Who made thee a prince and a judge over us? intendest thou to kill me, as thou killedst the Egyptian? And Moses feared, and said, Surely this thing is known"* (Exodus 2:14). He then spent 40 years in a desert wilderness living as a shepherd and it was at that time, that he learned the lowly ways of being a despised one.

> *"But God has chosen what the world calls foolish to shame the wise; he has chosen what the world calls weak to shame the strong. He*

has chosen things of little strength and small repute, yes and even things which have no real existence to explode the pretensions of the things that are – that no man may boast in the presence of God. Yet from this same God you have received your standing in Jesus Christ, and he has become for us the true wisdom, a matter, in practice, of being made righteous and holy, in fact, of being redeemed. And this makes us see the truth of scripture: 'He who glories, let him glory in the Lord"

(1 Corinthians 1:27-30 J.B. Phillips).

At a prophetic time in history, the Lord changed the standard for governing within His kingdom and He declared that the old ways shall be no more to the prince of his people.

"And thou, O deadly wounded wicked one, the prince of Israel, whose day is come, in the time of the iniquity of the end, thus saith the Lord Jehovah: Remove the mitre, and take off the crown; this shall be no more the same; exalt that which is low, and abase that which is high"

(Ezekiel 21:25-26 NAS).

> *The Lord was declaring that from now on there is a new order of ruling in his Kingdom and it is the way of lowliness and humility.*

This is prophetic because the Prince never wore both the crown and the mitre! The crown was for the prince and the mitre was the turban that the high priest wore. The Lord was declaring that from now on there is a new order of ruling in his Kingdom and it is the way of lowliness and humility. God does not want His priests or kings (his people) to operate through pride and arrogance anymore! We are a royal priesthood (1 Peter 2:9). The church of our Lord Jesus Christ is called to be kings and priests.

"And from Jesus Christ, who is the faithful witness, and the first begotten of the dead, and the prince of the [kings] of the earth. Unto him that loved us, and washed us from our sins in his own blood. And hath made us [kings] and [priests] unto God and his Father; to him be glory and dominion for ever and ever. Amen"

(Revelation 1:5-6).

"And hast made us unto our God kings and priests: and we shall reign on the earth"

(Revelation 5:10).

"For every high priest taken from men is appointed in service to God for the people, to offer both gifts and sacrifices for sins. He is able to deal gently with those who are ignorant and are going astray, since he is also subject to weakness"

(Hebrews 5:1-2 HCSB).

A priest must have compassion on the poor, needy, rebellious, and ignorant people in the world because he himself is surrounded by so many weaknesses. A king must be able to rule, make decisions and function as royalty. No more can he think of himself as a lowly beggar, an orphan, or a nobody, but he must see his calling to be a king. *"He raises the poor out of the dust, and lifts the needy out of the ash heap, that He may seat him with princes, with the princes of His people"* (Psalm 113:7-8 NKJV). God is looking for the lowly, bruised, and broken to lift them out of the ash heap (garbage dump), then He, Father God makes them to sit with princes and to reign as a king. The problem is that if I grew up in a palace, then I can easily lack compassion on the poor, ignorant, and needy people in the world. Whereas if I grew up in poverty, then I can continue to live like a pauper, even though I am now to reign and conduct myself as a king. Hence, the solution is to embrace the grace of God to repent of all pride and hardness of heart and to be poor in spirit (see Matthew 5:3). The word poor actually means that you can only beg and if someone does not help you, you will not be able to survive in life. This involves a total change of heart and this is the true essence of repentance.

> *God is looking for the lowly, bruised, and broken to lift them out of the ash heap (garbage dump), then He, Father God makes them to sit with princes and to reign as a king.*

Once the heart has been changed, it is now time to change your mind. You can now rule as a king, this is the essence of being renewed in the spirit of your mind (see Ephesians 4:23). Am I too high to be poor and needy before my God or am I too low to be a king unto my God? Putting on the new man or true self involves putting on Christ and taking off the old false self with all of its sinful, fallen, and corrupt ways of thinking (see Eph. 4:22-24, Romans 13:14). Unbelief is called an evil heart in the sight of God and if I only see myself as a beggar, then I do not believe in my high calling as a king in Christ Jesus (see Eph. 1:18-23, 2:6). We are seated with Him in the heavenly places right now!

I never really saw how important it is to see myself in my heart as a lowly beggar (poor in spirit) and to also see myself as an exalted son of God in Christ Jesus! If we do not see ourselves as exalted sons and daughters in Christ, then the earth will not be able to bear up under our ruler-ship. Those ruler-ships which we are meant to reveal Christ in such as: parent, employer, president, chancellor, teacher, apostle, prophet, pastor, doctor, and etc. *"For three things the earth is disquieted for and for four which it cannot bear: for a servant when he reigns"*, (Prov. 30:21-22a). How we see ourselves will be revealed by our speech and actions towards those under us. This is the hour for lowly, meek servants on the inside, but exalted kings on the outside that can lead and govern in Christ, whatever their sphere of rule involves. It is a tremendous truth that the Lord chooses the lowly, despised people of this world to be his greatest leaders and servants. The difficulty and crisis comes when these lowly, despised ones carry their mind-set of being a beggar into their Royal Calling.

There was a movie called, *"The Prince and the Pauper"* (1937): In Tudor England, two boys are born on the same day in the most different circumstances imaginable. The boy Tom is the son of a vicious criminal John Canty; while the boy Edward VI is a prince and the heir of King Henry VIII of England. One boy grows up in poverty and hungering for something better for himself and his family; while the other boy is isolated in luxury and with a strong curiosity about the outside world. When they are youngsters, they meet and are astounded by their striking resemblance to each other. As a prank, they exchange clothes, but the Captain of the Guard mistakes the prince for the pauper and throws him out of the palace grounds. Tom is unable to convince anybody except for the Earl of Hertford of his identity. Everyone else is convinced that he is mentally ill. In this movie the true Prince Edward exchanges his clothes with the Pauper, Tom Canty. Now, because of the mistaken identities, Tom, the Pauper becomes Edward the Prince and Edward the Prince becomes Tom the Pauper.

This movie is a very good illustration of the problem that many believers face as they are enthroned with Christ to operate and to rule in His name and in His authority on His behalf. In the movie, the prince lived in a king's palace his entire life and the pauper lived in an impoverished neighborhood all his life. The prince was what would be called a spoiled child, that had a hard attitude towards others; but the pauper even though he had a drunk for a father, was trained by a godly priest how to be compassionate towards others. One had to learn compassion and the other had to learn how to rule and reign with courage and dignity.

Moses tells God, who am I that you would use me, use someone else. I cannot speak and I am a stutterer. He greatly struggled to enter into the call of God that was now to be fulfilled in and through him. God has a set time for everything under the sun, but being renewed in the spirit of our mind (see Ephesians 4:24) includes being changed in the way we see ourselves as a prince and true child of the King of Kings. Some of the necessary preparation to be trained to rule as one of the King's sons is to learn how to deal with rejection, slander, and misunderstanding; while at the same time learning how to increase in compassion. Moses's time in the very Presence of the Lord imparted to him the virtue of meekness. This became a great asset in dealing with the failures and sins of the people that he led in the wilderness for 40 years. The Lord loves to take the lowly insignificant people of the world and make them Princes and Rulers over others, as the following Scriptures testify:

> *"Then the word of the Lord came to Jehu the son of Hanani against Baasha, saying, Forasmuch as I exalted thee out of the dust, and made thee prince over my people Israel; and thou hast walked in the way of Jeroboam, and hast made my people Israel to sin, to provoke me to anger with their sins; Behold, I will take away the posterity of Baasha, and the posterity of his house; and will make thy house like the house of Jeroboam the son of Nebat"*
>
> (1 Kings 16:1-3).

> *"He raiseth up the poor out of the dust, and lifteth the needy out of the dunghill; That he may set him with princes, even with the princes of his people"*
>
> (Psalm 113:7-8).

> *"The sentence is by the decree of the watchers, the decision by the word of the holy ones, to the end that the living may know that the Most High rules the kingdom of men and gives it to whom he will and sets over it the lowliest of men"*
>
> (Daniel 4:17 ESV).

> *"Let this mind be in you, which was also in Christ Jesus: Who, being in the form of God, thought it not robbery to be equal with God: But made himself of no reputation, and took upon him the form of a servant, and was made in the likeness of men: And being*

*found in fashion as a man, he humbled himself, and became
obedient unto death, even the death of the cross. Wherefore God
also hath highly exalted him, and given him a name which is
above every name"*

(Philippians 2:5-9).

God makes us to reign as Princes, but Princes need to understand
the ways of the Lord and they need to learn the ways of royalty, i.e.
how to live as a royal priest and king.

*"The prince that lacketh understanding is also a great oppressor, but
he that hateth covetousness shall prolong his days"*

(Proverbs 28:16).

*"Under three things the earth is disquieted and quakes,
And under four it cannot bear up: Under a servant when he reigns,
Under a [spiritually blind] fool when he is filled with food,
Under an unloved woman when she gets married,
And under a maidservant when she supplants her mistress."*

(Proverbs 30:21-23 AMP)

According to the above scripture, there are four things that the earth
cannot bear up under, one of them is a servant when he reigns. God
gave the earth to the children of men (see Psalm 115:16) and He will
not take it back from them until it is the time, but for now it is ours
to govern. Therefore, when a slave rules, he has to be retrained how to
think as a Ruler and not as a slave.

> *...there are four things that the earth cannot bear up under,
> one of them is a servant when he reigns.*

Here are some more examples of lowly individuals that were chosen
to be great leaders:

GIDEON

"And I said unto you, I am the Lord your God; fear not the gods of the Amorites, in whose land ye dwell: but ye have not obeyed my voice. And there came an angel of the Lord, and sat under an oak which was in Ophrah, that pertained unto Joash the Abiezrite: and his son Gideon threshed wheat by the winepress, to hide it from the Midianites. And the angel of the Lord appeared unto him, and said unto him, The Lord is with thee, thou mighty man of valour. And Gideon said unto him, Oh my Lord, if the Lord be with us, why then is all this befallen us? and where be all his miracles which our fathers told us of, saying, Did not the Lord bring us up from Egypt? but now the Lord hath forsaken us, and delivered us into the hands of the Midianites. And the Lord looked upon him, and said, Go in this thy might, and thou shalt save Israel from the hand of the Midianites: have not I sent thee?"

(Judges 6:10-14)

Gideon was afraid, unbelieving and not thinking of himself as a leader at all. He had such a thick mindset of being a beggar, being the least and not being worthy of God using him. He had to put away his mindset and put all of his confidence in the word of the Lord.

DAVID

"Now therefore so shalt thou say unto my servant David, Thus saith the Lord of hosts, I took thee from the sheepcote, from following the sheep, to be ruler over my people, over Israel: And I was with thee whithersoever thou wentest, and have cut off all thine enemies out of thy sight, and have made thee a great name, like unto the name of the great men that are in the earth. Moreover I will appoint a place for my people Israel, and will plant them, that they may dwell in a place of their own, and move no more; neither shall the children of wickedness afflict them anymore, as beforetime, And as since the

time that I commanded judges to be over my people Israel, and have caused thee to rest from all thine enemies. Also the Lord telleth thee that he will make thee an house. And when thy days be fulfilled, and thou shalt sleep with thy fathers, I will set up thy seed after thee, which shall proceed out of thy bowels, and I will establish his kingdom. He shall build an house for my name, and I will stablish the throne of his kingdom for ever. I will be his father, and he shall be my son. If he commit iniquity, I will chasten him with the rod of men, and with the stripes of the children of men: But my mercy shall not depart away from him, as I took it from Saul, whom I put away before thee. And thine house and thy kingdom shall be established for ever before thee: thy throne shall be established forever. According to all these words, and according to all this vision, so did Nathan speak unto David. Then went king David in, and sat before the Lord, and he said, Who am I, O Lord God? and what is my house, that thou hast brought me hitherto? And this was yet a small thing in thy sight, O Lord God; but thou hast spoken also of thy servant's house for a great while to come. And is this the manner of man, O Lord God? And what can David say more unto thee? for thou, Lord God, knowest thy servant. For thy word's sake, and according to thine own heart, hast thou done all these great things, to make thy servant know them. Wherefore thou art great, O Lord God: for there is none like thee, neither is there any God beside thee, according to all that we have heard with our ears. And what one nation in the earth is like thy people, even like Israel, whom God went to redeem for a people to himself, and to make him a name, and to do for you great things and terrible, for thy land, before thy people, which thou redeemedst to thee from Egypt, from the nations and their gods? For thou hast confirmed to thyself thy people Israel to be a people unto thee forever: and thou, Lord, art become their God. And now, O Lord God, the word that thou hast spoken concerning thy servant, and concerning his house, establish it forever, and do as thou hast said"

(2 Samuel 7:8-25).

David, like so many of God's choice leaders had a very small opinion of himself. When Saul told him to be the King's son-in-law, he was shocked that he would even suggest such a thing.

> *"And Saul said to David, Behold, my elder daughter Merab, her will I give thee to wife: only be thou valiant for me, and fight Jehovah's battles. For Saul said, Let not my hand be upon him, but let the hand of the Philistines be upon him. And David said unto Saul, Who am I, and what is my life, or my father's family in Israel, that I should be son-in-law to the king?"*
>
> (1 Samuel 17: 17-18)

David, who grew up in rejection and loneliness watching sheep, used a word for broken that meant to be broken, to be crushed in penitence with a contrite heart.: Strong's H7665 – shabar (see Psalm 51:17).

Solomon, on the other hand, who grew up in a king's palace used a word for broken that meant sadness, sorrow and affliction. It is Strong's number H5218 – naka. "A merry heart doeth good like medicine, but a broken spirit drieth up the bones" (Proverbs 17:22) and "The spirit of a man will sustain his infirmity: but a wounded spirit who can bear" (Proverbs 18:14).

JOSEPH

Joseph was used mightily as a leader for the people and was another person that sought nothing for himself only desiring to be a faithful servant. One chosen by God will always have the call of greatness on their life. The servants the Lord chooses to be great are the least of men and therefore these men that are least now enter into true greatness. These servants must learn how to function as a lowly and humble king. A lowly, humble beggar is no problem for them to accept, but a lowly, humble king is quite another story. Father God looks for broken and lowly vessels that He can use and He makes them vessels of honor. He trains their hands for war, He makes them kings unto Himself.

All the sacrifice that God requires is a broken and contrite heart within a person.

> *"The sacrifices of God are a broken spirit: a broken and a contrite heart, O God, thou wilt not despise" (Psalm 51:17). This tender and broken heart will treat others the way that it desires others to treat them. "Therefore all things whatsoever ye would that men should do to you, do ye even so to them: for this is the law and the prophets"*
> (Matthew 7:12).

Once I had a vision and I saw in the spirit two girls both about 21 years old. On the outside, they both looked so different. The first one looked very nicely dressed with beautiful clothing and the other looked very poorly dressed with cheap torn clothing. The first one looked very well-mannered, poised and she knew exactly how she should respond to people. The other one did not know the "proper" way to speak and she had no understanding of manners. The one is the type of daughter that most parents would be very proud to have. The other one is a daughter that some parents could be ashamed of. The one was very careful who she had for friends and the other one did not pay attention to her friends. The one was not sexually promiscuous on the outside. The other one did not even understand that sex before marriage is considered a sin in the eyes of God.

I saw this vision and then suddenly I could see them in the sight of heaven. The first one that appeared as very stunning, dignified, and glamorous on earth was ugly, hard, insensitive and uncaring on the inside. Therefore, in the sight of heaven, she was extremely ugly because the real person is the invisible person of the heart (see author's book, The Lamb's Heart for a full unveiling of this). The second one had a beautiful, soft heart on the inside and therefore she was lovely in the sight of the invisible heavenly world.

For many years I saw how extremely important the one quality of the hidden man of the heart was in order for God to use us in His service. Sadly, I did not see how extremely important the other quality of having a renewed mind as a dignified prince is under the highest ranking Emperor in the universe. A prince should not and must not carry himself in the sight of others as anything less than the Emperor's child!

> *Before the prince can act like a prince,*
> *he must see himself as a prince and this is called*
> *the renewing of the mind for a believer.*

Before the prince can act like a prince, he must see himself as a prince and this is called the renewing of the mind for a believer. In today's world, there are a lot of pauper's who act and talk like a prince (because of their pride); on the other hand there are a lot of prince's that act and talk like paupers, because of ignorance, fear, and unhealed issues of their heart. Many times I would drift back into my false self with all of its discouragement, irrational ways of thinking and speaking. I needed to start to live my life out from my true self (the new man) and to put off the false self (the old man). In order for one to put on Christ, we need to see who Christ is and see the all sufficiency of Christ within our own heart and life. When things happen to us that trigger old memories and thought patterns, we can react out of the false self, instead of acting from the center of our being and living in the true self. As we take our place as sons and daughters of the King, we will then live from the true self or what is called a new creation and in this realm, Christ is all.

> *"But when that which is perfect is come, then that which is in part shall be done away. When I was a child, I spake as a child, I understood as a child, I thought as a child: but when I became a man, I put away childish things. For now we see through a glass, darkly; but then face to face: now I know in part; but then shall I know even as also I am known"*
>
> (1 Corinthians 13:10-12).

That which is perfect is the fullness of God in the face of Christ Jesus. When we see the face of Christ, we are changed from one realm of glory into another realm of glory. *"But we all, with open face beholding as in a glass the glory of the Lord, are changed into the same image from glory to glory, even as by the Spirit of the Lord"* (2 Corinthians 3:18). As we behold as in a mirror, the one who is our very life (Christ), we are changed into the same image of God. As I focus on myself, I am actually seeing my false self or my fallen self and I will begin to focus more on my insecurities, sins, failures, and insufficiencies. We are told to put on the new man or the new self (true self) who is made in the very image and likeness of God and reveals true holiness.

> *"That, regarding your previous way of life, you put off your old self [completely discard your former nature], which is being corrupted through deceitful desires, and be continually renewed in the spirit of your mind [having a fresh, untarnished mental and spiritual attitude], and put on the new self [the regenerated and renewed nature], created in God's image, [godlike] in the righteousness and holiness of the truth [living in a way that expresses to God your gratitude for your salvation]"*
>
> (Ephesians 4:22-24 AMP).

One of the main reasons that we speak as a child is because we do not see the one, who is the perfect Man, which is living inside of us.

One of the main reasons that we speak as a child is because we do not see the one, who is the perfect Man, which is living inside of us. One day we will completely see what He is and what He is inside of His body the church. When this day of fullness comes we will no longer know in part, but we will know fully even as we are known by God. There are many times that we are to go from glory to glory by beholding more of his infinite fullness in us! Father God's plan is to bring forth at this very hour mature believers that can reveal his full measure of grace and glory in the world. A child speaks, thinks, and understands as a child; but a mature son, thinks, speaks, and understands as a mature adult. It is time to put away childish things that hold us back from truly knowing God in his fullness.

"And of his fulness have all we received, and grace for grace"
(John 1:16).

"And I am sure that, when I come unto you, I shall come in the fulness of the blessing of the gospel of Christ"
(Romans 15:29).

"Which is his body, the fulness of him that filleth all in all"
(Ephesians 1:23).

"And to know the love of Christ, which passeth knowledge, that ye might be filled with all the fulness of God"
(Ephesians 3:19).

"Till we all come in the unity of the faith, and of the knowledge of the Son of God, unto a perfect man, unto the measure of the stature of the fulness of Christ"
(Ephesians 4:13).

"Beware lest any man spoil you through philosophy and vain deceit, after the tradition of men, after the rudiments of the world, and not after Christ. For in him dwelleth all the fulness of the Godhead bodily. And ye are complete in him, which is the head of all principality and power"
(Colossians 2:8-10).

The Apostle Paul said "I am sure, that when I come to you I shall come in the fullness of the blessing of the gospel of Christ", (Romans 15:29). It delights the Father to know that His children have appropriated the fullness of blessing that the gospel brings to them. We are living in a day of fullness and we should not settle for anything less than the full measure of Christ at this hour. My dear brothers and sisters strive with me by the grace of God to enter in to the rest of the Lord where we can cease from all our own works and allow His complete full work be accomplished within us.

CHAPTER 17
CONCLUSION

As a concluding thought, I want to remind you that Jesus Christ, the son of God has come to earth to reveal his Father to us as he said, *"And this is life eternal, that they might know thee the only true God, and Jesus Christ, whom thou hast sent. I have glorified thee on the earth: I have finished the work which thou gavest me to do. And now, O Father, glorify thou me with thine own self with the glory which I had with thee before the world was. I have manifested thy name unto the men which thou gavest me out of the world: thine they were, and thou gavest them me; and they have kept thy word."* (John 17:3-6) Eternal life is to know the Father and his son. Jesus also said that no one can come to the Father, except through him (see John 14:6). One of the main goals that the Son of God had on earth was to bring back the Father's sons and daughters. Father is waiting for his children to return to him, but they can only return through being joined to the Son. It is in him that we find the Father and discover his tremendous love for us. He actually loves us just as He loves his son Jesus. *"I in them, and thou in me, that they may be made perfect in one; and that the world may know that thou hast sent me, and hast loved them, as thou hast loved me."* (John 17:23.) Jesus wants the entire world to know that the Father has loved us just as he loved Jesus.

When we are reborn into the family of God through the blood of Jesus that was shed for mankind, it was because God deeply desired that we experience his love as our true Father in heaven. The father in the story of the prodigal son said to the older brother, it is necessary that we are merry and be glad. In other words, we must have a party because your brother has returned home (see Luke 15:32). The angels rejoice in heaven when one sinner returns to God in repentance. *"Likewise, I say unto you, there is joy in the presence of the angels of God over one sinner that repenteth."* (Luke 15:10) All of heaven rejoices when a sinner returns to their heavenly father's loving arms. *"I say unto you, that likewise joy shall be in heaven over one sinner that repenteth, more than over ninety and nine just persons, which need no repentance."* (Luke 15:7)

There are many of God's children that are thinking that God does not want to be bothered with them. Maybe they never had a father that cared for them or maybe they have failed over and over as a Christian and now they feel it is too late. As we get ready to pray the following prayers, please allow the arms of Father God to embrace you, kiss you, welcome you, and restore you back into his family. Jesus is standing at his right hand interceding on your behalf. The Father is running to meet you and love you with a pure unselfish love.

Please pray the following prayers out loud while acknowledging the pure, holy, and loving presence of God. Also please pray each of these prayers out loud and slowly. Do not just pray these as a ritualistic, religious type of prayer. Instead, slowly invite God the Father to come to you and heal every part inside of your soul and to put his healing love and power in you. Welcome His real Presence with every single one of these prayers that you pray.

Before we pray these prayers, I want to mention that I have prayed with thousands of people, similar prayers to the ones listed here. I have seen thousands of lives changed by the presence of Father God. One unfortunate truth seems to be that many of the wounded people that I pray with have no idea that their wounds are usually somehow connected to their father. To help us understand the vital role of fathers in our lives and the deep emotional or physical wounds that accumulate due to an abnormal, unhealthy, and lack of relationship with dad; I will quote from an article by Kenny Luck on the Christian Post called "Fatherhood: man's highest calling?".

"Today, virtually every societal problem, social injustice, and behavioral abnormality can be traced back to absent, delinquent, misbehaving, drunk, or sexually immoral dads who don't respect or understand their enormous calling."

Then Mr. Luck continues, considering these statistics from the Girl Scout Research Institute:

- "90% of all women want to change at least one aspect of their appearance, and only 2% of women think they are beautiful.
- 81% of 10 year-olds are afraid of being fat
- A girl is being bullied every 7 minutes
- Every 15 seconds a woman is being battered
- 50% of music videos portray women as sex objects, victims or in a condescending way
- 1/4 college women have an eating disorder
- 1/3 girls between 16-18 years of age say that sex is expected of them at their age if they are in a relationship"

(Luck 2014)

So many people are suffering from many problems in their life, in areas such as: marriage, thought-life, family, relationships, body, and etc. After receiving prayer major healing begins. In my ministry, I pray personal prayers for many individuals and we discover months later that they experienced a radical change in their life.

Many that come for prayer are literally shocked when they experience the deep inner change that takes place after receiving something as simple as a blessing from a spiritual father. I believe that Father God is so delighted when a spiritual father can stand in His name and place, to speak blessing, healing, and life into these individuals.

We just had a Couples Seminar and at the end of the Seminar, the Father said that my wife Marie and I were to speak a parental blessing over any couple that did not receive a real (not religious) blessing from their parents for any reason at their wedding. What followed shocked both Marie and me. First, most of the couples came forward to be blessed. Second, just as soon as we started to speak and pronounce the blessing of God, the Father , demons started to leave people. Thirdly, it was revealed to me that the demons were leaving simply because we were breaking the curses that these dear couples had lived under through just a word of blessing. Once the curse was removed, the demons had no more legal right to remain.

First of all, Father God, come and fill the room of this person reading this book now. We welcome your Presence and Spirit. Come, Holy Spirit, and bring us into the very Throne of Grace.

Now let us begin with the prayers:

I come now through the blood of Jesus Christ. His blood has opened the veil and made a way for me to enter into the holiest of all. I now enter boldly to receive mercy and to find all the necessary grace for my healing, deliverance, and wholeness in the name of Jesus (Hebrews 4:16). Thank you, Lord! Thank you, Father, for receiving me and welcoming me into your very Arms of love. Father, fill me and pour your Holy Presence into me even while I am praying these prayers. Thank you!

PRAYER TO RELEASE GOD FROM ALL DISAPPOINTMENT AND TO ASK FORGIVENESS FOR JUDGING HIM AND NOT TRUSTING HIM

Father, I release you for any disappointment that I have ever had in my life and especially if I blamed you inside of my heart. Please forgive me for judging you for not doing what "I thought" you should have done. Release me from all the effects of my judgments. Thank you, Father God.

PRAYER TO FORGIVE AND TO RELEASE EVERYONE THAT DISAPPOINTED US IN OUR LIFE

Dear Father, right now in the name of Jesus, I forgive (name of person) and I release him/her for (action). I forgive him/her for the action that he/she did and I release (name of person) for the dishonor and disappointment he/she caused me to feel emotionally. I forgive and release (name each person and self and God) for every disappointment. I will not carry any more disappointments in my heart or soul. Father, please cleanse me from the effects of every disappointment.

PRAYER TO RELEASE EVERY PERSON
THAT DISHONORED ME

Father, right now I completely release and forgive every person (name anyone whose name or face is strong in your memory) that dishonored me and made me feel like my life had no value and that I was worth nothing.

PRAYER TO FORGIVE AND RELEASE MOTHER

Father God, forgive me for not honoring my mother in any area. I also forgive and release my mother for not making me feel special and giving me honor. I also release my mother for (list anything that comes to your mind). Thank you, God, for complete cleansing from any abuse or shame from my mother.

PRAYER TO BE RELEASED
FROM ANY INNER OR OUTER VOWS
(thoughts or words spoken against me, my life, and my circumstances)

Father, I take back every negative word I spoke against myself, every time I thought or spoke that I did not want to be alive, wishing I was never born, or any other time I wished I could escape my present world. I declare now that I break all agreement with death, death wishes and vows against myself and my life. 'I WANT TO BE WHOLE AND I WANT TO LIVE.' From this moment on I will live and fulfill my purpose in life.

PRAYER TO BE RELEASED FROM ALL SELF PITY
AND TO RELEASE EVERY PERSON
THAT ABANDONED OR DESERTED ME

Father, I forgive and release everyone that abandoned or deserted me as a child and as an adult. I completely release them for not covering me and being there for me to share my heart and feelings with. I also ask you, Father God, to forgive me for inviting self-pity to cover me and to comfort me. From this moment, my God and Father will be a wall and fire around me and not self-pity. I repent and renounce all self-pity in my life, in the name of Jesus Christ.

PRAYER TO FORGIVE AND RELEASE EVERY PERSON THAT WOUNDED; ABUSED OR HURT ME IN ANY WAY

Father, I repent for all bitterness in me and I renounce and repent for every attitude connected with bitterness such as unforgiveness, resentment, revenge, anger, hate, violence, murder, and including murder with my tongue in Jesus' name. I completely release and forgive everyone for every debt and offense against me. Release me now, Father God, from all bitterness in my soul. Thank you, Lord. I ask for your power now to come into my soul and to fill me with love and supernatural strength to go on and live without any bitterness. Thank you, Lord.

PRAYER TO BREAK ALL UNGODLY SOUL-TIES

Lord Jesus, I repent for committing any fornication or having sexual relations outside of marriage (name any names that you remember). I also repent for allowing others to control or manipulate me through my fear. I repent now for daydreaming and for being in any relationship (even with a group or church) that was not from you. Release me, Lord Jesus, from all ungodly ties with any person or group and cleanse me from all the effects of these ungodly soul-ties. Thank you, Lord Jesus. Restore my soul now and make me whole and send back to all others any fragments of their soul that belong to them. Now, I command any spirits that attack me through these ungodly ties to leave me now in the name of Jesus Christ. Amen. Thank you, Lord.

PRAYER TO RELEASE EVERY PERSON FROM ANY DEBT THAT I HAVE HELD ONTO REGARDING THEM

Right now, since Jesus Christ shed his sacred blood and said "Tetelestai" (John 19:30), which means "it is finished" and "the debt is paid in full", I forgive and release every single person that raped, abused, hated, misused, controlled, manipulated, rejected, lied, slandered, criticized me, and all other evil done to me in any way in my entire life; from the time that I was conceived in my mother's womb until this present moment. (If any names come to your mind while you are slowly praying, speak them out loud.) I cancel every single debt that they owe me, because their debt has been paid in full by the blood of Jesus Christ. Amen.

PRAYER TO BE RELEASED FROM ANY BELIEFS THAT I HELD ONTO IN MY LIFE THAT WERE GRIEVING TO THE HOLY SPIRIT (Ephesian 4:30a)

Holy Spirit, I ask you to forgive me for grieving you by believing lies, false teachings, beliefs that made me proud or harsh towards others, or any teachings that were contrary to the clear teachings of the Holy Scriptures. I also repent of any fear towards you, the other Comforter; the one called to walk along side of me. I receive you now to fill me afresh and anew with your pure and holy Presence. Thank you so much for cleansing me and filling me now.

PRAYER TO BE RELEASED FROM ALL UNRIGHTEOUS AND HARD JUDGMENTS THAT I EVER MADE ON ANY PERSON FOR ANY REASON

Since you, Lord, forbid me to make unrighteous judgments on any one, because there is only one Lawgiver and Judge. I ask you to forgive me and release me for judging anyone. I now choose to have mercy on them instead of judgment, because mercy is what I desire for myself, so I now give it to all others. (see Matthew 7:1-3, Romans 2:1-2, Romans 14:12-14, Luke 6:35-38, James 12:1-11, etc.)

PRAYER FOR REBELLION DUE TO MISTRUST OR CONTROL FROM AUTHORITY FIGURES

Father God, I repent from all rebellion in my life. I forgive every authority figure (parent, teacher, government official, employer, and etc.) that was controlling, dominating or abusive to me. From now on I choose to submit to every authority that you have put in my life and to trust you, Father God, to cover me and give me godly wisdom. Please release me from all the effects of rebellion in my life. I also break witchcraft from manifesting through me anymore. Father, I ask you to give me your lowly, submissive love. Thank you, Lord Jesus.

PRAYER TO BE RELEASED FROM ALL FEAR

Father God, you have promised me that I would serve you in holiness, righteousness and without fear all of the days of my life You have not given me a spirit of fear, but love, power and a sound mind and that perfect love casts out fear. So, right now I repent of all fear and I break agreement with fear and I release every person that made me fearful, in Jesus' name. Cleanse me from fear now. This moment I enter into your arms of perfect love. I embrace your love and receive you, Father God, in me. Thank you for loving me so much.

PRAYER TO BE RELEASED FROM ALL HATRED TOWARDS WEAKNESS IN MY BLOODLINE AND IN ME

Father, I repent for all hate towards weakness in my ancestors and in my own life. I renounce this form of hate as a deep inner hatred for the Lamb of God. I want to love the Lamb of God, so from this moment on I break agreement with all hatred towards weakness in me and in my bloodline. Forgive me, Father, for all the times that I was mean, hard or unfeeling towards my family or friends. From this moment on, I will humble myself and I will ask every person that I was hard towards to please forgive me. Father, cleanse me from all the effects of this hate in me. I choose the heart of the Lamb to be my heart.

Now, as the final prayer I will pray for you and I just ask that you pray this out loud as if I was there praying over you right where you are now.

PRAYER:

"Dear Father, I welcome you to come to your son/daughter now and embrace him/her. We thank you for filling the room/car/building where he/she is now, in Jesus' name. I remit all of your sins and I retain the power of sin over your life, under the order of Melchizedek. You are free from the effects of sin in your family bloodline and in you. I release the goodness of God over you now. Receive His goodness, presence, and love. You are released from all the effects of sin through the all-powerful blood of God and you are now free, in Jesus' name. I ask that you allow me to stand in the place of any man (father, pastor, brother, etc.) that abused you and to please release us men for not covering you and honoring you, but instead for uncovering you. Please forgive all of us for not showing you what a godly man looks like. Release us for all the deep pain, disappointment and hurt that we (male leaders) have caused you in your life. I break off of you the lie that tells you, that "you don't deserve to be alive", "you must prove it". I break this lie forever and I command all the stress, grief, pain, sorrow, and death to leave your soul and to go out of your body right now. I release the peace of God into your spine and your nervous system and I command fear and tension to leave your body now. Dear child, every thought that you think and every word that you speak is important because it comes from you and you are important. You are not a mistake, you are not an accident and you are not a burden. You are a blessing. Even if you were not your parent's plan; you were definitely God's plan. He ordained that you would be here for such a time as this. Receive His love and healing and gentleness into your innermost being.

You, beloved one, are special; not because of anything that you have or have not done, but because you are. Just because you are here on earth and Father God truly deeply loves you. I give you back the honor that others have taken off of you. Right now receive your honor back and enter into your true self in the name of Jesus Christ. Gentleness is the key to greatness, so would you please forgive your parents if they did not show you gentleness, especially when you knew that you deserved correction. Father God, I ask that you pour your healing balm of pure, kind love into the memories of this dear child of yours. Thank you for healing the pain and defilement in his/her very memories. Receive His cleansing from all that shame and defilement that others have put wrongfully upon you. I release you from that deep inner feeling that you are just a little, helpless, and confused child that does not know what to do. I release you into your manhood/ womanhood and into your destiny as a man/woman of God. I call you out of your false self and I call you forth into your true self. Father, I ask that you disconnect your child from any trauma that has them still tied to the second heavens. Release them from any demonic link to the second heavens that the evil one has been using to trigger them due to their traumatic memories. Thank you, Father, for breaking this link now and destroying all of its power through the blood of your Son. In Jesus' name, I command the spirits of trauma to leave now with stress and torment. Father, release your dear child from all the effects of trauma in his/her life. You are now loosed from infirmity, sickness, self-hatred, and rejection. Resurrection power (see Ephesian 1:19-20) is flowing into your body and you are being released now from tumors, arthritis, and mental infirmities. Cancer is dissolving now in the name of Jesus Christ and his resurrection power and life is entering into that part of your body. Your organs are receiving the healing power of the Father. You are honored and special and you are blessed child of God. Receive the pure love and compassion of your Heavenly Father. Allow him to wrap his arms around you just like the father of the prodigal son ran to him, embraced him, kissed him, and completely restored him. Even if you might have been on the garbage dump in life, your true Father in heaven set you with princes and has taken you off the garbage dump of life. You are loved and restored by the Father himself.

"He raises up the poor out of the dust, lifts the needy out of the dunghill [garbage dump] that he may set him with princes, even the princes of his people"

(Psalm 118:7-8).

Now enter into the status of a king, enthroned in the very Son of God, seated with Him in the heavenly places! I bless you in the name of the Redeemer, our Lord Jesus Christ. Amen."

Your servant in Christ,
Greg Violi

BIBLIOGRAPHY:

1. Buechner, Frederick (1985): The magnificent defeat.
   San Francisco: Harper & Row.
2. Lynch, James J. (2000): A cry unheard. New insights into the medical consequences of loneliness.
   1st. Baltimore MD: Bancroft Press.
3. Mosby, Inc (2009): Mosby's medical dictionary. 8th ed. Edinburgh: Mosby.
4. Parish, Fawn (1999): Honor. What love looks like.
   Ventura Calif.: Renew.
5. Rinck, Margaret Josephson (1990): Christian men who hate women. Healing hurting relationships. Grand Rapids Mich.: Pyranee Books (Lifelines for recovery).
6. Watson, G. D.: Pure Gold: Kingsley Press.
7. Winter, Jack; Ferris, Pamela (1997): The homecoming. Unconditional love: finding your place in the Father's heart. Seattle, WA: YWAM Pub.
8. Holloran, Pat: I will not leave you as Orphans. 1st. 2010: Harvest House International Ministries.
9. Sports Illustrated (1995): Bo Jackson.
10. Hegstrom, Paul (2006): Broken children, grown-up pain. Understanding the effects of your wounded past. 2nd ed.
    Kansas City Mo.: Beacon Hill Press of Kansas City.
11. National Center for Fathering: Extent of Fatherlessness.
12. Darby, Gordon: Father Wounds.
13. Chambers, Oswald (1992): My Utmost For His Highest //
    My utmost for His Highest. An updated edition in today's language the golden book of Oswald Chambers.
    Grand Rapids Mich.: Discovery House Publishers.
14. Luck, Kenny (2014): Fatherhood: Man's Highest Calling?
    In CP Opinion.

OTHER LIFE CHANGING BOOKS
AVAILABLE FROM PASTOR GREG VIOLI:

Depression and Introspection: Healing for the diseased mind:
This book explains root causes for depression and how the disease of introspection affects millions. Greg shares from the Word of God how depression blocks a person from living in the presence of God and how a you can walk in freedom it.

The Lamb's Heart
This book is a thorough revelation of the spiritual heart of man and the heart of God. It contains many truths concerning brokenness in the father's heart and how to allow the father to heal your own brokenness.
There is a tremendous revelation about how and why God always looks at the heart of man.

The King's Holy Beauty
This book is a revelation of the secret mystery hidden in the heart of Father God. This revelation from the Holy Spirit is to unveil the beauty of God`s holiness. Since this book has been published there have been many testimonies of the changed lives of the people who have read it.

Whose Image and Which mind
This book discusses the differences between heavenly and earthly wisdom, the heavenly image and the earthly demonic image. Through this book you can discover the splendor of living life through the heart of the Lamb of God! Living a life after God´s heavenly design and being fed from the river of divine wisdom!

Called to be kings and Priests

In this book the purpose of a godly father and husband are revealed
through the scriptures. It is also reveals how to live out God's divine
design and purposes of a man practically. Through revelation from God's
Word you will also learn how to heal wounds created by men not
fulfilling God's calling on men.

A Heavenly Victorious life

The Spirit of the ascended Christ desires to come inside of a believer
and reveal himself. When we allow him to reveal himself through us;
it produces a heavenly life, a life that is always abounding in victory.
Greg describes the real life of the ascended, exalted Lord
and how we can abide in the fullness that he offers.

The Key to Staying in Love

God desires mercy more than any sacrifice that man can offer.
In any relationship, the most desirable attributes are kindness,
mercy, and love. When a person allows appearance or possessions
to take first priority in a relationship, judgements and hardness replace
a heart attitude of kindness and love. The love of God cannot abide
where there is hardness of heart. In this small booklet, you can learn
how judgements operate and how to guard yourself from
such destructive attitudes.

71695380R00133

Made in the USA
Middletown, DE
27 April 2018